DEDICATION

To the man who's tired of average—who knows he was made for more. You're not a spectator. You're a warrior.

These Special Ops are for you.

15 MISSIONS GUARANTEED TO STRENGTHEN YOUR FAITH & TRANSFORM YOUR LIFE TODAY

SPECIAL OPS FOR MEN

JEFF JERINA

AUTHOR OF *FAITH WITHOUT FEAR* & *CUT THROUGH THE NOISE*

Special Ops for Men

For more information or to schedule an interview, contact:
Jeff@JeffJerina.com

ISBN 979-8-9951062-2-7 (paperback)
ISBN 979-8-9951062-0-3 (ebook)

Sales of this book support the ministry of Jeff Jerina and companies. Helping others go the next level in their faith, business, and personal life with interactive training, speaking, coaching, group training, courses, books, online tools, and more, including *The Jeff Jerina Show* podcast and community. **Learn more at www.JeffJerina.com.**

Published by: Olive Tree Publications, Wylie, TX
Printed in the United States of America

For discounts on books, bulk discounts, live or virtual training with Jeff, or to book Jeff for a speaking engagement, please visit **www.JeffJerina.com.**

DOWNLOAD YOUR BONUS GEAR FREE!

To say thank you for buying this book, I want to give you some exclusive bonus gear—100% FREE.

This gear is reserved for readers only. It's not available anywhere else. You'll receive:

- **Mission Tracker & Battle Plan** - A tactical tool to track your objectives, progress, and wins.
- **Special Ops Warrior Code** - A bold declaration to anchor your identity and what you stand for.

TO DOWNLOAD, GO TO:

JeffJerina.com/Books/SpecialOpsforMen/Resources

CONTENTS

SECTION III

MULTIPLY YOUR IMPACT

INTRODUCTION

Five hundred meters of open terrain. Hostile fire from three directions. Equipment failure. Communications down.

In live combat, this calls for quick and decisive action. No meetings, no long talks. You assess, adapt, and move. Push through or get pinned down. Simple as that.

Your everyday life? It's no different.

You know what I'm talking about—when you realize that going through the motions isn't working anymore. When half-hearted faith and weak leadership are a guaranteed path to failure. Maybe that moment hasn't hit you yet. Or maybe you're in the thick of it right now, fighting to become the man God created you to be.

Either way, you picked up this book for a reason. Maybe it's curiosity, maybe it's a prompting from a close friend, or maybe it's something deep in your gut that's waiting for you to live your true self.

And so right now, I want you to know—this isn't just another book to collect dust on your shelf. I've got plenty of those. This one's different.

This is your **battle plan.**

Your **field guide.**

Your **wake-up call** to live with conviction and courage.

THIS IS WAR

And right away, I want you to know two things:

1. I've never served in the military.
2. But I've been impacted by those who have.

From the stories of my grandfather, a World War II vet...To conversations with my father-in-law who was a F-4 navigator in the Air Force...To conversations with high-ranking officers and Special Ops commanders on my podcast...To the deep respect I carry for every person who's stepped into combat...

I've learned this: **Every man needs a mission.**

Whether you've worn a uniform or not, **you were born into a war**—the likes none of us have ever seen. And whether you like it or not, you're already on the front lines.

That's right! As a Christian man—a warrior for Jesus Christ—you've been called to:

- Fight for your faith.
- Defend your family.
- Push back the darkness.
- Never surrender.
- Live with honor.

BORN FOR BATTLE

So why the military theme?

Because deep down, every man responds to the call of battle. You feel it when you watch *Hacksaw Ridge, Braveheart, Gladiator,* and *Unbroken.* You don't just watch those films—you feel them deep down, calling the warrior within.

That's not a coincidence. It's something **God hardwired into you the moment you were born**—to be more than a passive observer. To stand. To fight. To lead.

But here's the problem: **most Christian men have settled.**

We've gone passive in a war that demands action. We've played defense when God has called us to take the offense. To charge forward rather than retreat. And to stand firm rather than surrender.

That ends today.

NEVER SURRENDER

Special Ops for Men gives you a battle-ready, mission-based approach to strengthen your faith, awaken your soul, and transform your life—starting now.

God doesn't mince words about your calling:

> *Be on your guard; stand firm in the faith; be courageous; be strong.*
> **—1 Corinthians 16:13**

These aren't suggestions.
They're not motivational slogans or ideas.
They're **commands—direct orders** from your Commander in Chief, God Himself.

And His message is clear: You were made for more than spiritual mediocrity. More than just getting by. More than watching from the sidelines.

You were made for battle.

It's time to move out.

Your orders are waiting.

HOW THIS BOOK WORKS

Every warrior needs a battle plan—and this briefing is yours.

This book isn't designed to be read and forgotten. It's meant to be used, to be executed—one short mission at a time. Each chapter (or mission) gives you a clear, actionable step you can execute immediately to improve some area of your life, whether it's your faith, health, relationships, mindset, discipline, or legacy.

WHY MISSIONS?

I call these 'missions' because I can't challenge you face-to-face over a cup of coffee, on a phone call, or during a workout. And let's be real: if we didn't know each other, would you even listen? Probably not.

Because that kind of challenge—really any challenge—is hard to receive from someone you don't know.

But as your brother in Christ and a fellow soldier in the trenches, I'm not here to lecture you. I'm here to equip and empower you—to put real tools and strategies in your hands. That's why these aren't just chapters. They're missions. Actionable, boots-on-the-ground operations you can start running today.

They're not fluff.
They're not religious busywork.
They're practical. Tactical. And effective.

MISSION STRUCTURE

Each mission follows the same tactical format, so you always know exactly what to do:

- **Mission Introduction**. Quick overview that sets the context and explains why this mission matters.
- **Mission Purpose**. The "why" behind the mission—how it will impact your life.
- **Mission Plan**. Clear objectives laid out in simple, doable steps.
- **Mission Tools**. The resources you'll need (don't worry—you already have most of them).
- **Estimated Completion Time**. A realistic timeframe (most missions take just minutes).
- **Mission Fuel**. Scripture, quotes, and motivation to keep you powered up.

- **Mission Debrief**. Space to reflect, track progress, and capture the lessons you've learned.

This structure isn't filler. It's designed to take you from **understanding → action → reflection.** And that rhythm is where transformation happens.

WHAT TO EXPECT

Each mission is:

- **Short and doable** (some take less than 60 seconds)
- **Clear in purpose** (you'll know exactly what to do)
- **Flexible** (fit them into your life whenever you can)

And each one ends with a **Mission Debrief**—a short section where you can capture key takeaways, track your wins, and stay accountable. There's nothing fancy here. No essays. No journaling novels. Just honest reflection and practical application.

I've organized these missions in a specific order because they build on each other. But you're free to execute them in whatever sequence you want.

At the end of the book, there's a **Final Mission Debrief**—which is a bird's-eye view of what you've accomplished, how you've grown, what you've learned, and what to work on next.

Following the Final Mission Debrief, you'll find the **War Room**—an optional group study guide. It's a tactical set of discussion questions to use after you've personally completed the missions. Use it to review your mission results with men who've run the same ops.

READY FOR IMPACT

Each mission is strategically designed to fit your life— no matter how busy or rushed you are. You won't need to clear your calendar, get special clearance, or hit pause on your daily responsibilities.

You just need the **courage to act**.

Most missions take minutes to complete, but their impact lasts a lifetime. They're not designed to crush you— they're made to activate you. To wake up the warrior God put inside you. Some will stretch you. That's intentional. Because growth happens at the edge of your comfort zone.

These missions aren't just about what you do— they're about who you're becoming and the legacy you'll leave behind.

So, let's cut to the chase:

You don't need more information.

You need transformation.

Let's get to work.

GEAR UP

YOUR TOOLS & REINFORCEMENTS

No soldier goes into battle unarmed.
And you won't either.

Here are some **free tools and support systems** I've created to help you succeed in every mission.

THE MISSION TRACKER + BATTLE PLAN

If you're looking for that extra edge or some additional firepower to push your faith and life to the next level, I've created a FREE *Special Ops Mission Tracker and Battle Plan* to help you ace each mission. This FREE tool helps you:

- Record your victories.
- Track your progress.
- Capture deeper insights.
- Stay consistent with your growth.

Get yours at:

- JeffJerina.com/Books/SpecialOpsForMen/Resources

THE WARRIOR CODE

Every elite warrior follows a code—a creed that defines his purpose, his values, and his commitment to the battle. Yours is no different.

Inside this book, you'll find a link to the **Special Ops Warrior Code**—a daily declaration of who you are in Christ and what you stand for. This code isn't just words on a page. It's a battle plan to rally around when the fog of war descends on your life. I encourage you to:

- Read it daily.
- Memorize it over time.
- Live by it with conviction.

Get your printable or mobile version at:

- JeffJerina.com/Books/SpecialOpsforMen/Resources

Download it for free and keep it in front of you as a daily reminder of who you are and what you stand for:

JOIN THE BROTHERHOOD OF MEN

History has proven that **a lone soldier is vulnerable, but a team of warriors is unstoppable**.

Join the Brotherhood—a free online community where you can:

- Share wins and challenges without judgment.

- Get encouragement from men fighting similar battles.
- Unlock **3 Bonus Missions**
- Get accountability from other brothers in Christ.

Join for free at:

- JeffJerina.com/Books/SpecialOpsforMen/Resources

THIS BOOK IS FOR EVERY MAN

Don't let the title of this book intimidate you.

You don't need military training or a theology degree to carry out these missions.

What you do need… is courage.
Courage to act. Courage to fight. Courage to finish.

Whether you're:

- On the front lines of business,
- A dad leading the charge at home,
- Active duty or a veteran,
- Serving in ministry or retired, playing golf—

You're in the fight. And this book is your playbook.

The missions are clear.
The gear is in your hands.
The brotherhood has your back.
No excuses.

No retreat.
No surrender.

YOUR ORDERS

Turn the page. Start Mission 1.

The enemy isn't waiting—so why should you?

Lock in.

Gear up.

And let's move out.

SECTION I

STRENGTHEN YOUR FOUNDATION

MISSION 1

RECHARGE YOUR BATTERY

Faith is the foundation of courage, the source of strength, and the anchor in the storm.
—We Were Soldiers

Low Battery: 5% remaining.

The warning light flashes on your screen. Your phone dims to save power. If you don't find a charger soon—total shutdown.

But what about your spiritual battery?

There's no notification when it hits critical levels. You just wake up one day and realize you're going through the motions. Prayer feels like dead air. Your worship time becomes something to get through so you can watch the game. And your Bible? Collecting dust.

I know because I've been there—looking great on the outside while feeling completely drained on the inside.

The harsh reality is that the world drains us constantly. Work demands more. Your family needs more. Your bills need paying. Texts need answering. Before you know it, you're spiritually running on fumes, and your relationship with God takes the biggest hit.

The most dangerous part isn't even how empty you feel—it's how normal that emptiness becomes. You adapt to operating at 2% spiritual battery until you forget what being fully charged even feels like.

But here's the good news: while your phone needs a complicated charging device, God designed your spiritual recharge to be simple. No cords. No gadgets. No monthly payments (can I get an Amen). The power source is right in front of you—your Bible. Every time you open it, you draw power straight from God Himself.

Your recharge starts the moment you open God's Word.

The power source is right in front of you—your Bible. Every time you open it, you draw power straight from God Himself.

MISSION PURPOSE

Mission: Read a passage of Scripture.

This mission is about getting charged up. It's more than a chore or a military assignment—it's your lifeline. Every time you open God's Word, you get recharged and refocused. This isn't fluff. This is fuel for the battles ahead. Here's why this mission matters:

- **Life gets noisy.** Scratch that, life gets *extremely* noisy, and God's voice can seem distant. Every time you open His Word, you're stepping into a conversation with your Creator—it's like a personal coaching session with the ultimate coach.
- **Reading Scripture is strength training for your soul.** When life hits with challenges or doubt, you'll be anchored in truth instead of getting tossed around by the storms of life.
- **You're building a habit.** Just five minutes a day can transform your life and make Bible reading automatic, like brushing your teeth.

Just think—you wouldn't step into battle without intel or orders—you'd be completely vulnerable. Yet, that's exactly what happens when we go through life without reading God's Word. We become easy targets.

Mission Objective: By the end of this mission, you'll have:

- **Connected with God**
- **Strengthened your faith**
- **Built a daily habit that's life-changing**

MISSION PLAN

Today's mission is straightforward: grab your Bible and start reading.

There's no pressure to analyze, overthink, or 'get it right.'

Just read.

Pick a passage and let it sink in.

If you're not sure where to start, try one of these:

- **Psalm 23** – God's guidance and care
- **John 1:1-5** – Jesus as The Word and The Light
- **Ephesians 6:10-20** – Spiritual strength for battle
- **Philippians 4:4-7** – Trading anxiety for peace

That's it. Just read and let God's Word do what it does best—transform you from the inside out.

MISSION TOOLS

Pick one of these tools and start now:

- Bible (physical copy)
- Bible app
- Bible website

ESTIMATED COMPLETION TIME

1 to 5 minutes.

But don’t be surprised if you want to go longer.

MISSION FUEL

Man shall not live on bread alone, but on every word that comes from the mouth of God.
—Matthew 4:4

Think of God's Word as your fuel and your direct line to the greatest Commander-in-Chief. God doesn't just want to hear from you—He wants to counsel and coach you in every aspect of life.

So, go ahead—open your Bible.

Read it.

Absorb it.

Let it recharge you.

MISSION DEBRIEF

Before you move on to the next mission, take a moment to reflect. Remember, the goal isn't perfection—it's progress.

1. What passage of Scripture did you read?

2. How long did it take you?

3. On a scale of 1 to 10 (10 being the easiest), how easy was this mission to complete?

4. What challenged you the most during this mission?

5. What did you learn about yourself? About God?

6. What was the result of this mission?

7. What would you do differently next time?

MISSION 2

ARM YOURSELF WITH TRUTH

Victorious warriors win first and then go to war, while defeated warriors go to war first and then seek to win.
—Sun Tzu

Your boss drops a surprise deadline. A health problem hits out of nowhere. Temptation strikes when your guard is down. Life doesn't wait for you to be ready—and neither does the enemy.

Here's the deal: when you're unprepared, you get steamrolled.

Think about the quarterback who shows up on game day out of shape. The soldier who waits until bullets are flying to check his gear. Or the guy at work who tries to wing it and fumbles under pressure. Different battles, same problem: no preparation.

Your spiritual life works the same way.

Every day brings attacks—some obvious, some hidden, like a sniper tracking you from miles away. If you're not ready, you'll get blindsided. Every time.

Look, we're playing the most important game there is—life itself. Not just to survive or win by the world's standards, but to win God's way. And to help you claim victory, God hasn't left you defenseless. He's given you the ultimate weapon: His Word.

God hasn't left you defenseless. He's given you the ultimate weapon: His Word.

In Ephesians 6, Paul breaks down the armor of God piece by piece. Out of all that gear, **the sword of the Spirit, which is the word of God** (Ephesians 6:17) stands alone. It is the only weapon that can both shield your mind and strike at the heart of the enemy.

When you commit Scripture to memory, you're not just storing random words in your brain. You're arming yourself with a weapon that you can draw any time—to cut through Satan's lies, combat the world's corruption, and strike down your own worst impulses.

Remember Jesus in the wilderness? He didn't argue. He didn't panic. He didn't try to outsmart the devil. He simply quoted Scripture—and the enemy had no answer.

If Scripture was powerful enough for Jesus, it's powerful enough for you and me.

So, let's put it to work.

MISSION PURPOSE

Mission: Lock one verse into memory.

It's your tool when temptation hits, doubt creeps in, or discouragement bears down. Memorize it. Deploy it. And when life attacks, you won't fold.

Remember: God's Word is your weapon, your anchor, and your fuel. Commit this verse to memory, and you'll *always* have something to rely on in the heat of battle.

Mission Objective: By the end of this mission, you'll have God's Word ready to deploy at a moment's notice, equipping you to:

- **Stand firm.** Strengthen your faith in the storm.
- **Strike and defend**. Use Scripture as both your offensive and defensive weapon.
- **Build endurance**. Train your mind to rely on God's Word automatically in everyday battles.

MISSION PLAN

Your task is to **memorize a Bible verse.** That's it, one verse. It can be any verse you choose. If you're unsure where to start, here are a few suggestions:

- Be strong and courageous. Do not be afraid; do not be discouraged, for the LORD your God will be with you wherever you go.
  —Joshua 1:9 NIV
- The Lord *is* my shepherd; I shall not want.
  —Psalm 23:1
- The Lord is my refuge and my fortress; My God, in Him I will trust.
  —Psalm 91:2
- I press on toward the goal to win the prize for which God has called me heavenward in Christ Jesus.
  —Philippians 3:14 NIV

How to Memorize a Bible Verse:

- **Read it** out loud several times.
- **Write it down** in a notebook or on a sticky note.
- **Break it into** small sections and repeat them.
- **Say it** before you go to bed and when you wake up.
- **Review it** throughout your day.
- **Pray and apply** it to your life.

Don't overthink it—just start. The more you practice, the easier it gets.

MISSION TOOLS

- Bible or Bible app
- Bible website
- Index card, paper, or phone notes
- Pen (if you're writing it down)

If you need some extra help memorizing Scripture, check out my *Shortcut to Scripture Memory* course at:

- JeffJerina.com / Courses / ScriptureMemory

ESTIMATED COMPLETION TIME

1 to 5 minutes.

Reality check: That's faster than scrolling your social media feed. One small investment for eternal impact.

Did you know that **you can memorize a Bible verse faster than checking Facebook?** Studies show that most people spend over two hours a day scrolling through stuff that has no bearing on their lives. But here's what will—in the same amount of time it takes to read one social media post, you can memorize Scripture. That's not just a quick win—that's eternal impact.

MISSION FUEL

This Book of the Law shall not depart from your mouth, but you shall meditate in it day and night, that you may

observe to do according to all that is written in it. For then you will make your way prosperous, and then you will have good success.
—Joshua 1:8

As you can see, this verse hits different when you understand what real success looks like. For years, I thought success meant money, status, and climbing the corporate ladder. I chased all that stuff until I finally figured out what God was really saying here.

True success starts with knowing God's Word, living it out, and trusting Him to guide your path. Not the world's version of success—God's version.

This mission isn't just about *reading* God's Word—it is about *living it.* And that starts with locking it into your mind and heart.

True success starts with knowing God's Word, living it out, and trusting Him to guide your path.

Time to execute.

Choose your verse.

Memorize it.

Arm yourself with the truth—God's truth.

You've got this!

MISSION DEBRIEF

Take a moment to reflect on this mission. To help track your growth, please answer these questions honestly.

1. What verse did you memorize?

2. How long did it take you to memorize it?

3. On a scale of 1 to 10 (10 being the easiest), how easy was this mission to complete?

4. What challenges did you face?

5. How will you review this verse regularly?

6. How has this verse helped you?

7. What will you do differently next time? *Try a new memorization method? Choose a longer verse? Say it in prayer more often?*

MISSION 3

LOCK IN GOD'S WORD

The more you sweat in peace, the less you bleed in war.
—General Norman Schwarzkopf

Up to this point, you've been building your arsenal—reading God's Word, memorizing it, and making it part of your daily routine. But here's what separates the warriors from the wannabes: locking biblical truth into your mind where it makes the most impact.

Because right now, your brain is enemy territory until you take it back. Think about it—your mind is your command center. It's where most (if not all) of your battles are won or lost before they ever begin.

And here's the reality: a weak mind leads to weak decisions. However, a strong mind—one that's rooted in God's truth—leads to discipline, confidence, and faith. And every day, the devil launches attacks with some of his heaviest ammo: fear, doubt, lust, apathy, and pride. Most of those hit you before you even go to lunch. Thus, if you *don't* control your thoughts, they *will* control you.

That's why God commands us to be intentional about what we focus on:

> *Do not conform to the pattern of this world, but be transformed by the renewing of your mind.*
> **—Romans 12:2**

Translation: the warrior who meditates on God's Word carries a weapon no enemy can overcome.

So, how do you renew your mind? Simple. You meditate on God's truth—chew on it, wrestle with it, let it reshape how you see and do everything.

Think of it like tactical training. A soldier doesn't just read the manual once. He studies it, thinks through scenarios, and applies what he's learned until it changes how he operates. **You do the same with Scripture—you meditate on God's Word until His truth rewires your thinking.**

MISSION PURPOSE

Mission: Meditate on God's Word.

The real battle doesn't start with your hands—it starts in your head. That is so important to understand, because your thoughts control your choices, and your choices—whether good or bad—shape your life.

That's why this mission builds on everything you've done so far. You've been reading God's Word. You've been memorizing it too. But now it's time to go deeper—to plant Scripture so deep in your mind that it begins to transform who you are and how you live.

The real battle doesn't start with your hands—it starts in your head.

Here's why this mission is critical:

- **Reclaim Your Mind**. If you let doubt, fear, or negativity take charge, they'll wreck your life. Meditating on Scripture resets your mind to think like God thinks. To view things from His perspective, the eternal perspective (2 Corinthians 4:16-18).

- **Build Unbreakable Strength**. Just like lifting weights builds muscle, dwelling on God's Word builds inner strength. It gives you the backbone to stand strong when life gets tough. And brother, if you're like me, you've experienced that.

- **Eliminate Weakness**. A mind filled with truth leaves no space for worry, self-doubt, or temptation. God's

Word becomes the shield that blocks the enemy's attacks.

- **Master Self-Control**. The more you focus on God's truth, the stronger and more disciplined you become.

Bottom line: Your mind runs everything. Load it with garbage, and you'll collapse. Load it with God's truth, and you'll be unshakable.

Mission Objective: Train your mind by meditating on God's Word until it becomes second nature.

Now it's time to move from purpose to action. Here's the plan for today's mission.

MISSION PLAN

Choose one verse to meditate on today. If you don't have one in mind, start with one of these:

- Be on your guard; stand firm in the faith; be courageous; be strong.
  —1 Corinthians 16:13

- But his delight is in the law of the Lord, and on his law, he meditates day and night. He is like a tree planted by streams of water, which yields its fruit in season and whose leaf does not wither—whatever he does prospers.
  —Psalm 1:2-3

- Finally, brothers and sisters, whatever is true, whatever is noble, whatever is right, whatever is pure, whatever is lovely, whatever is admirable—if anything is excellent or praiseworthy—think about such things.
  —Philippians 4:8

Choose any verse you like. Lock it in. Treat that verse like an order you're training to obey—not a thought you skim once and forget. As you memorize it, make it personal: swap in words like *I, me,* and *my* so it speaks directly to you. Try this with something like Psalm 1:2–3. Instead of reading "But *his* delight is in the law of the Lord…", *say it as* "But *my* delight is in the law of the Lord, and on his law *I* meditate day and night. *I* am like a tree planted by streams of water…whatever *I* do prospers."

When you frame Scripture this way, it doesn't just stay on the page—it sinks into your identity and becomes your marching orders. Below is a short, battle-tested routine to make it stick.

- **Lock In.** Find a quiet place, away from distractions. This is battle-prep—so, treat it seriously.
- **Chew on It.** Read the verse slowly and really dig in. Ask yourself: What is God saying? What does each word mean? How does this impact my life? Let the verse roll around in your head until it clicks.
- **Make It Real.** Picture yourself living this truth. How would this change your day? Your decisions? Your thoughts? Your actions?

- **Wrestle with It.** Ask the hard questions: How does this apply to my life right now? What needs to change?
- **Carry It with You.** Write it down. Take a screenshot of it and store it in your phone. Put it where you'll see it on a regular basis—your wallet, computer screen, phone, car, gym bag, or mirror.
- **Live It Out.** Ask yourself throughout the day: How does this verse change the way I respond to what's happening right now?

This isn't passive reading. This is deep thinking. It's how you train your mind to be strong, focused, and locked onto God's truth.

MISSION TOOLS

- A Bible
- A notebook or phone notes
- A quiet place to reflect
- A reminder system – set an alarm, put a sticky note on your mirror—whatever it takes to keep God's Word rooted in your mind.

To help you with this, I've put together a *Shortcut to Scripture Memory* course that gives you a simple, proven system to memorize Scripture faster and actually retain it. You can find it at:

- JeffJerina.com/Courses/ScriptureMemory

ESTIMATED COMPLETION TIME

5 to 10 minutes.

As you execute this mission, please remember that it's not about checking a box—it's about training your mind for long-term success.

MISSION FUEL

I have hidden your word in my heart that I might not sin against you.
—Psalm 119:11

When you **store God's Word inside you**, it becomes your weapon against everything life throws at you.

Lock it in.

Live it out.

Put it into action.

The time is now.

MISSION DEBRIEF

After completing the mission, answer these:

1. What verse did you meditate on?

2. What word or phrase stood out the most?

3. Did this mission help you feel more focused and confident? Why or why not?

4. On a scale of 1 to 10, how easy was it to stay focused?

5. What distractions made it hard to meditate? *Phone, stress, thoughts, etc.*

6. What did you learn about yourself? About God?

7. How has this mission helped you?

8. What will you do differently next time? *Meditate longer? Choose a new verse? Apply it to a specific situation?*

MISSION 4

CEASE FIRE

Sometimes it is better to be a warrior in a garden than a gardener in a war.
—Gladiator

Guys like us know how to grind. How to roll up our sleeves and get stuff done. We can go all day without stopping. But being still? That's totally different. It feels weird and uncomfortable—like trying to speak a foreign language you've never learned. It seems impossible.

I get it. I'm the same way. Ask me about my week, and I'll tell you about a project I just finished, a problem I solved at work, or my yard that I finally got around to mowing. We define ourselves by what we accomplish, not by who we are or whose we are.

Here's the problem: in combat, if you never call a ceasefire, you eventually run out of ammo and energy. You burn out. The same thing happens in life.

Let's be real—when was the last time you called a buddy and said, "Man, I had the best time alone with God today?" It doesn't happen. Instead, we talk about our jobs, our kids' games, the latest sports scores, maybe even our workout routine. Now, there's nothing wrong with any of that, but it does reveal something about us.

The harsh reality is that the world around us—even the church sometimes—celebrates the hustle, the grind, and the never-stop mentality. We're told that real men are always productive, always moving forward, and always achieving (or at the very least, should be).

But when was the last time you just stopped, **called a ceasefire**, and listened to God?

Not the quick prayer at the stoplight. Not half-listening during worship while thinking about your lunch plans. Not reading a Bible verse while your mind is already jumping ahead to your to-do list.

I'm talking about total silence—just you and God.

If that makes you a little uncomfortable, join the club. Being still feels weird to most of us. It feels unproductive, maybe even like wasted time. But here's something I've had to learn the hard way: silence (being still), whatever you want to call it, isn't weakness. It's discipline.

In 2018, I had a lot on my plate. I just launched my podcast, I was running two businesses, and writing my second book, *Cut Through the Noise: 4 Steps to Joy, Peace, and Freedom.* Turns out, I was fighting for my own peace without even knowing it. Looking back, spending time with God wasn't even on my radar. Why not? Because I was so caught up in building my life that I forgot to include God in it.

But in my mind, I was crushing it, especially since I was so busy. Yet, I had forgotten the most important thing: to slow down and spend time with God. That's when this verse hit me:

> *Be still and know that I am God.*
> **—Psalm 46:10**

Notice God didn't say, "Stay busy and know that I am God" or "Check off your to-do list, get back to me when you have some time, and then know that I am God." No, He said, **"Be still."**

When we never pause or slow down, we miss what God is trying to tell us. The constant noise of life drowns out that still, small voice we need most. Notifications blow up our phones. Podcasts fill our ears. Social media feeds never stop scrolling. And all those meetings, they never end. As a result, our minds fill with distractions. Our shoulders carry the weight of stress. Our spirits run on fumes, and then we're left wondering, "Why do I feel so distant from God?"

But something changes when we call a **ceasefire**—we step into strength. We give God the time and space to speak to us personally, to refresh us, and to guide us. The direction we've been frantically chasing often comes, not through more effort, but through more silence.

Today's mission is easy to understand but challenging to do, especially if you're always busy, always on the move. Call a ceasefire. Take 1 to 5 minutes to sit in silence—no music, no phone, no distractions—just you and God.

The direction we've been frantically chasing often comes, not through more effort, but through more silence.

You don't need more noise. You need more time with God.

MISSION PURPOSE

Mission: Rest in God's presence.

If you're always rushed, always running, always doing, you'll never hear what God is saying. That's why learning to be still matters.

- **Stillness Builds Strength**. Even the best warriors know when to pause, reload, and reset.
- **God Speaks in the Quiet**. Elijah didn't hear God in the wind or the fire, but in the gentle whisper (1 Kings 19:11–12).

- **Rest Is a Weapon**. The enemy wants you burned out and distracted. But a man who learns to rest in God's presence cannot be moved.
- **Slow Down to See Clearly** – When you're always running, you miss God's direction. Silence brings focus, clarity, and peace.

This is where real warriors reset, recharge, and prepare for what's next.

Mission Objective: Allow God to restore your soul and renew your strength as you rest in His presence.

MISSION PLAN

Find a quiet place and spend 1 to 5 minutes in complete silence. Here's your step-by-step plan:

- **Turn Off Distractions**. Silence your phone, turn off your computer, step outside, or find a quiet room.
- **Start with a Simple Prayer**. Ask God to clear your mind and speak to your heart. Try: *"Lord, I'm here. Please speak to me."*
- **Be Still and Listen**. No words, no rushing. Just you in the Lord's presence.
- **Focus on Scripture**. Let God's Word—even just one verse—guide your thoughts. Try Psalm 46:10, Isaiah 40:31, or Matthew 11:28-30.

- **Write Down Your Thoughts**. If the Lord brings something to mind, write it down and think about it.

Remember: You're not trying to force anything to happen. You're just making yourself available for God to work.

MISSION TOOLS

- A quiet space
- A Bible
- Something to write with
- A timer - so you're not watching the clock.

For that extra firepower, check out my *Cut Through the Noise* book. It walks you through four simple, yet practical steps to help you break through all the noise and distractions of life, eliminate all the hurry, and connect with God on a deeper level. You can find out more and get your own copy at:

- JeffJerina.com/Books/Cut-Through-the-Noise

ESTIMATED COMPLETION TIME

1 to 5 minutes.

Or however long you want. Although this mission is short, it can change everything. Don't confuse the brevity of the mission for the magnitude of results. And don't mistake the silence for inactivity—God is working.

MISSION FUEL

Come to me, all you who are weary and burdened, and I will give you rest.
—Matthew 11:28

"Silence is God's first language; everything else is a poor translation." —Thomas Keating

Think about that for a second. God speaks best through silence. All the noise around us—the TV, the phone calls, the constant chatter—all of these make it harder to hear what He's really saying.

Here's what you need to remember: Silence isn't wasted time. It's worship time. When you sit still with God, you're not being lazy. You're not being unproductive. You're being proactive. You're being wise. You're making space for God to speak to you the way He wants to, the way you need Him to.

So, **stop moving and start listening.**

God is already there waiting for you.

MISSION DEBRIEF

After you finish this mission, take some time to think about and answer these questions:

1. Was it hard to be still? Why or why not?

2. Did you have any thoughts, feelings, or Scripture that came to mind? What were they?

3. On a scale of 1 to 10, how easy was this mission?

4. What distractions tried to pull your focus away?

5. What did you learn about yourself? About God?

6. How has this mission helped you?

7. What will you do differently next time? *Will you rest longer in God's presence, make this a daily habit, or focus on a specific Bible verse?*

MISSION 5

CLEAR THE DEBRIS

The enemy thrives in darkness; drag him into the light and his power breaks.
—Anonymous

Imagine you're hiking a mountain trail with some of your buddies. Word is, the view from the top is well worth the climb. But halfway up, you realize your backpack is loaded with rocks that you picked up at the beginning of the hike. You think, *'Why did I pick up these stupid rocks!? Whose idea was this? Oh yeah, it was mine.'*

Once that reality sets in, you notice that your friends are moving at a faster pace while you're falling behind—sweating and struggling with every step you take.

That's what unconfessed sin does to a man's life. It weighs you down when you're trying to move forward.

Every guy reading this knows what I'm talking about—that one thing that keeps tripping you up. A temptation or sin that keeps dragging you down. Maybe it's anger that explodes when you least expect it. Maybe it's looking at stuff online you know you shouldn't. Maybe it's the way you talk to people when you're stressed. Whatever it is, you know it's there. And God knows it too.

> *Therefore, since we are surrounded by such a great cloud of witnesses, let us throw off everything that hinders and the sin that so easily entangles. And let us run with perseverance the race marked out for us.*
> **—Hebrews 12:1**

Think about it this way: A boxer doesn't carry extra weight into the ring. When he prepares for combat, he strips down to what's essential. Soldiers do the same thing. Everything else—that's irrelevant to the battle—gets left behind because it could mean the difference between victory and defeat.

That's what this mission is about—getting rid of that extra weight. You're going to identify one piece of debris in your life—that one sin that's been slowing you down—and you're going to finally clear it out. Before we move on, I want you to know that this isn't about beating yourself up. Rather, this is about getting free so you can run the race God has for you.

So, today we're going to deal with it. Not tomorrow. Not next week. Not when you have the time. But right now.

MISSION PURPOSE

Mission: Confess your sin to God.

Why does this mission matter? Because carrying sin is like running with a heavy chain around your legs. It doesn't work. It slows you down, keeps you from moving forward, and eventually trips you up.

- **But here's the truth: sin loses its grip when you drag it into the light.** The devil wants you to keep secrets because secrets give him power. But the moment you confess, that stronghold begins to break, and the enemy starts to lose his grip on you.
- **Freedom starts with honesty.** You can't fix what you keep pretending isn't broken. Real strength isn't about acting tough—it's about being honest and facing your struggles head-on. Own them. Call them out. Take action. That's how you break free and move forward.
- **God is ready to meet you there.** He's not looking down at you in disappointment. He's waiting to lift the weight off your shoulders the moment you hand it over to Him. Scripture says: If we confess our sins, He is faithful and just to forgive us our sins and to cleanse us from all unrighteousness (1 John 1:9).
- **You were made for more than this.** That sin you're carrying—it's holding you back. It's keeping you from becoming the man God created you to be. It's time to drop it and move forward.

Mission Objective: Drag your sin into the light by confessing it to God. Break the enemy's grip and walk in the freedom Christ has already won for you.

> **Real strength isn't about acting tough—it's about being honest and facing your struggles head-on.**

MISSION PLAN

Here's what you're going to do:

- **Get Real About What's Holding You Back.** Find a quiet spot and ask yourself: *"What's the one sin I keep wrestling with?"* Don't overthink it. Whatever comes to your mind first, that's probably it.
- **Write It Down.** Grab a piece of paper and write it out. Be as specific as you can. Don't write something vague or general like, "I sin sometimes." Rather be as detailed as you can. Jot down something like, "I lose my temper with my kids," "I'm so quick to judge others," or "I have lustful thoughts about..." The goal in this step is to name your stronghold.
- **Confess It Out Loud.** Talk to God about it. He already knows what you're dealing with, but saying it out loud breaks the power of shame and secrecy.

- **Make the Turn.** Repentance isn't just saying you're sorry. It's admitting you were wrong, then going the opposite direction. Tell God you're done with this and you need His help to change.
- **Destroy the Evidence.** Rip up that paper, burn it, so you can never retrieve it again. This shows you're serious about letting it go.
- **Fill the Void.** Find a Bible verse that speaks truth over your situation. Write it on a piece of paper, save it in your phone notes, or keep it as a daily reminder on your calendar. Whatever you decide, make sure to keep it where you'll see it. If you need more help with this step, go back and look at Mission 3.

MISSION TOOLS

- A pen and a piece of paper
- Your Bible or Bible app
- A quiet, private space
- Courage—the enemy will try to talk you out of this

ESTIMATED COMPLETION TIME

5 to 10 minutes.

That's it. Less time than it takes to scroll through your social media feed. Yet most of us will carry that weight for years rather than spend five minutes being honest with God.

MISSION FUEL

If we confess our sins, he is faithful and just and will forgive us our sins and purify us from all unrighteousness.
—1 John 1:9

Then I acknowledged my sin to you and did not cover up my iniquity. I said, "I will confess my transgressions to the LORD." And you forgave the guilt of my sin.
—Psalm 32:5

Repent, then, and turn to God, so that your sins may be wiped out, that times of refreshing may come from the Lord.
—Acts 3:19

Thanks be to God, who gives us the victory through our Lord Jesus Christ.
—1 Corinthians 15:57

Before you roll out, remember that confession isn't about shame. It's not about beating yourself up or thinking you've blown it. God didn't rescue you so you could stay stuck. He set you free so you can experience real freedom—starting today. Here's what Galatians 5:1 says: It is for freedom that Christ has set us free.

Now, roll out and complete this mission knowing you don't have to haul this weight anymore.

MISSION DEBRIEF

Now that you've completed the mission, take a few minutes to answer these questions:

1. How did it feel to write down that specific sin and then destroy the paper?

2. What was the hardest part about confessing your sin or stronghold to God?

3. On a scale of 1 to 10 (10 being the easiest), how easy was this mission?

4. What truth from Scripture are you going to meditate on to replace the lie that sin was telling you?

5. How do you feel now compared to before you started this mission?

6. What's one practical step you can take this week to avoid falling back into this pattern?

7. How might this freedom impact other areas of your life?

SECTION II

FORGE MENTAL AND PHYSICAL DISCIPLINE

MISSION 6

MASTER YOUR MINDSET

Braver is he who overcomes his desires than he who conquers his enemies, for the hardest victory is over self.
—Marcus Aurelius

"It's all in your head."

That's what everyone kept telling me as I battled severe depression and thoughts of ending my life. They weren't completely wrong, but from 1997 to 2001 those words felt like salt on an open wound.

I was twenty-six years old when Body Dysmorphic Disorder (BDD) took over my life. What started as a quick glance at a scar on my hand turned into an obsession that consumed my every thought. I stared at that scar for hours every day, believing that because of *it* I was ugly, unlovable, and unworthy to live. All that negative thinking became a prison I built around myself, one mental brick at a time.

I still remember the breaking point. I was sitting at home alone, staring once again at the scar that had become my whole identity.

Then a question popped into my head from nowhere: *"What if it's not about the scar?"*

That question changed everything. For the first time in my life, I realized that my only path to real freedom was to surrender my life to Christ—and praise God I did!

Through counseling, a lot of prayer, and digging into Scripture, I discovered a truth that set me free: my mind is a battlefield. And until that moment, I had been fighting on the enemy's terms. Losing, I might add.

Your mind is a battlefield too.

This is what spiritual warfare looks like—the battle for your thoughts, your identity, and your future. And today, you're going to fight back and win. You're going to do that by identifying a lie Satan has been using against you and crushing it with God's truth.

Here's the deal: Every action you take starts with a thought. When that thought takes root, it shapes your decisions, which ultimately forge your destiny. The devil knows this. That's why his first attack always targets your thoughts. **If he captures your mind, he controls the mission.**

But there's hope. Scripture tells us in 2 Corinthians 10:5 to "take every thought captive and make it obedient to Christ." This isn't a casual suggestion—it's a direct order. And soldier, you're already equipped to carry it out.

If the devil captures your mind, he controls the mission.

I learned this lesson the hard way. For years, I let negative thoughts run wild in my head, telling myself I wasn't good enough, strong enough, or smart enough. Those thoughts became my reality because I never questioned them. But after I committed my life to Christ and got serous about prayer and reading God's Word, something clicked. I began to see that most of what I believed about myself was wrong—lies I'd accepted without a fight. So, I started pushing back. When a destructive thought tried to take hold, I'd stop and ask: *"Is this what God says about me? Does this line up with His truth?"*

What I learned was a total game changer. Those negative thoughts that had controlled me for years fell apart the moment I compared them to Scripture. Once I exposed those lies with God's truth, real freedom began. That's when I realized the power you and I have in this battle.

Your assignment: Identify one destructive thought pattern that's been draining your spiritual strength and replace it with the unshakeable truth of God's Word.

MISSION PURPOSE

Mission: Replace a negative thought or lie you've been believing with God's truth.

Why does mastering your mindset matter? Because the way you think shapes your life. For example:

- **Your Thoughts Control Your Life**. What you think about the most ends up influencing and guiding your actions. Think about it like this: the thoughts that you replay over and over become worn paths—or score marks—in your brain. Sooner or later, you'll end up walking those same paths in real life. Maybe you know someone who has been stuck in a dead-end job, a toxic relationship, or a spiritual rut simply because they can't imagine anything better.
- **You Get to Choose Your Response**. It's no secret that you can't control everything that happens to you. Life throws curveballs. But you can control how you respond, how you react to those situations. That split-second when you decide what to think about something? That moment has more power than most people realize. A job loss, a health scare, or a relationship that went south doesn't define you. How you respond to those things—that's what does.

- **God's Truth Wins Every Time**. Satan is constantly trying to mess with your head. And his biggest weapon is deception. Often, the lies he feeds you seem so innocent that you start believing they're true. But you have a defense: God's Word. Every time you deploy it, you cut through all the garbage the enemy has been dishing out. When you measure everything against Scripture, even the sneakiest lies lose their hold on you.
- **Mental Discipline Makes You Stronger**. The toughest guys I know win their battles upstairs (in their minds) before they ever face them outside (in the real world). Every time you take a negative thought or lie captive and replace it with God's truth, you're arming yourself for the next challenge.

Mission Objective: Walk boldly in freedom and renewed strength as God's truth takes root in your mind.

MISSION PLAN

Now that you understand the battlefield, here's how to win the war. Set aside five to ten minutes to confront a negative thought and replace it with God's truth. Here's your game plan:

- **Identify the Enemy**. What's the primary lie weighing you down? Write it down. Getting it out of your head and onto paper will rob it of some of its power. For me, it was: '*I am defined by my flaws.*' What is it for you?

- **Arm Yourself with Truth**. Find a Bible verse that combats that lie. When I battled body dysmorphic disorder (a severe form of body shame), 1 Samuel 16:7 became my lifeline: "Man looks at the outward appearance, but the Lord looks at the heart."
- **Create Your Counter-Attack**. Rewrite the lie as a statement of truth based on God's Word. Make it personal and in the active tense. Mine became: *'I am loved and valued by God for who I am, not by what I've done, and not by what I look like. My worth comes from my heart, which God sees as beautiful.'*
- **Declare It Out Loud**. Don't just read it—say it with authority. There's power when God's truth comes through your voice. Here's what I did: I would stand in front of the mirror, look directly at the scar I hated, and proclaim God's truth over myself.
- **Stay on Guard**. When that negative thought or lie returns—and it will—immediately fire back with your truth declaration. No waiting, no negotiating, no entertaining—just immediate replacement. This isn't a one-time fix; it's an ongoing battle. And one that you can win today!

As you carry out this mission, remember this isn't about positive thinking or self-help mantras. It's about aligning your mind with biblical reality—letting God's truth take hold in your mind and reshape how you see yourself and your circumstances.

For me, the scars haven't gone away—but their power over me and how I think about them did. By changing my thoughts, I've reclaimed the ground the enemy had taken from me.

And that same victory is available to you—one thought, one declaration, one battle at a time.

MISSION TOOLS

- **Something to Write With**. A journal, your phone notes, or a pen and paper.
- **Your Bible or Bible App**. Use one of these to help you find verses that speak truth over your situation.
- **A Quiet Space**. Somewhere you can think clearly without distractions.
- **Honesty.** You'll need the courage to identify those negative thoughts or lies that are weighing you down.

ESTIMATED COMPLETION TIME

5 to 10 minutes.

This mission is quick to complete but powerful in its impact. The real work happens when you practice this throughout your day.

MISSION FUEL

Listed below are a few examples of the lies that can trip you up in the battle for your mind. The truths paired with each one are your ammo—use them to push forward in your mission or to get unstuck when life feels too heavy.

Lie:
"I'm not good enough."
Truth:
I can do all things through Christ who strengthens me.
—Philippians 4:13

Lie:
"I'll never break this habit."
Truth:
If the Son sets you free, you will be free indeed.
—John 8:36
Truth:
The Lord is my rock, my fortress, and my deliver; my God is my rock, in whom I take refuge, my shield and the horn of my salvation, my stronghold.
—Psalm 18:2

Lie:
"God doesn't really care about me."
Truth:
Cast all your anxiety on Him because He cares for you.
—1 Peter 5:7

Lie:
"I've screwed up too much for God to forgive me."
Truth:
Therefore, there is now no condemnation for those who are in Christ Jesus.
—Romans 8:1

Lie:
"I'm alone in this fight."
Truth:
I will never leave you nor forsake you.
—Joshua 1:5

Listen up, soldier—your mind is the battlefield that determines everything else. The enemy wants to plant lies that will cripple you, but you've got the ultimate weapon: God's truth. Every time a lie tries to take root, hit it with Scripture.

Take control.

Stand firm.

Win the fight.

Now move out and complete the mission.

MISSION DEBRIEF

Before advancing to the next assignment, spend some time going through this mission debrief.

1. What negative thought or lie did you identify? How long has it been affecting you?

2. When you challenged this thought, what did you discover? Was it actually true?

3. What Bible verse or truth did you find to replace it? *Consider writing the entire verse here as well.*

4. On a scale of 1 to 10 (10 being the hardest), how difficult was this mission?

5. What made this mission challenging? What made it easier?

6. How will you remember to practice this mental switch throughout your day?

7. What did you learn about yourself? About God? About the power of your thoughts?

MISSION 7

ARMOR UP

The more you sweat in training, the less you bleed in combat.
—Richard Marcinko, Navy SEAL

You can have the best armor in the world, but if you're too weak to carry it, what's the point?

Think about that for a second. In Ephesians 6, Paul tells us to put on the full armor of God. He's not talking about physical gear, but the spiritual armor we need to fight spiritual battles. But here's what we often forget: you can't separate your physical condition from your spiritual readiness. When your body is weak or worn down, everything seems harder. When you're tired, it's tough to pray. When you're out of shape, spending time with your kids or serving others can wear you out fast. The bottom line: your physical strength helps fuel your spiritual strength.

When you train your body, you're not just building muscle. You're building discipline, endurance, and mental toughness. Whether it's extra push-ups, a run you've been putting off, or choosing to get off the couch and do something active, every rep trains your mind and spirit that you were made to advance.

You can't separate your physical condition from your spiritual readiness.

Yet most of us push our bodies like rental cars—hard, fast, and without much care. We ignore the warning lights and hope they'll keep running. We skip exercise because we're 'too busy,' or let's be honest—because we don't like pain. Instead of training ourselves, we watch athletes compete on TV and call it good. We tell ourselves, *"I'll take care of my health someday."*

But that 'someday' never comes. In many ways, we've turned our physical health into an afterthought.

Here's the reality—a soldier who neglects his physical condition won't last long in battle. The same is true for you in everyday life. And it's something Scripture warns us about. Paul writes in 1 Corinthians 6:19-20:

> *Do you not know that your body is the temple of the Holy Spirit who is in you, whom you have from God, and you are not your own? For you were bought at a price; therefore glorify God in your body…*

Read that again. Your body isn't just yours—it belongs to God. So, taking care of it isn't vanity. It's stewardship. It's preparing yourself for *whatever* He calls you to do, *whenever* He asks you to do it.

Think about it. If you're always tired, out of shape, or running on empty, how effective can you be as a dad? As a husband? As an employee? As a leader? As a man of God? Physical weakness doesn't stay in the gym. It shows up in other areas of your life as well—your attitude, your relationships, your resolve, and your faith. In other words, when your body struggles, everything else suffers too.

And that's exactly why this matters. God designed men to be strong—physically, mentally, and spiritually. But strength doesn't happen by accident. It's built through discipline, hard work, and pushing past your comfort zone. When you strengthen your body, you strengthen your mind. When you train yourself to push through physical pain, you're training yourself to push through spiritual battles as well.

When you train yourself to push through physical pain, you're training yourself to push through spiritual battles as well.

Today's mission: Move your body. Engage in some form of exercise that pushes you beyond your normal limits. Even if it's just a little.

If you already work out, add five more reps to your routine. If you don't, try doing ten sit-ups, five push-ups, or going on a fifteen-minute walk. It doesn't have to be extreme. It just has to be more than yesterday.

Because every time you push your body harder, you're not just building muscle—you're building discipline. You're also proving to yourself that you can accomplish difficult things. And that strength carries over into every area of your life.

MISSION PURPOSE

Mission: Push your body past its comfort zone today—no excuses, no shortcuts.

Here's what's on the line: A weak or tired body makes everything harder. With this in mind, here's why this mission matters:

- **Physical Strength Builds Mental Toughness**. The discipline it takes to push through a hard workout is the same discipline you need when life gets tough. One thing to remember is that when you train your body, you also train your mind.
- **You're Preparing for God's Mission**. Whether it's being a dad that's present and engaged in the lives of his kids, serving in your community, or just having the energy to do what needs to get done, a strong body helps you live out your purpose.
- **Self-Control Starts with Your Body**. This virtue of self-control (of controlling your actions) is the first

one my son learned when he started his martial arts training in Taekwondo. And it's essential, because if you can't control your actions, albeit what you eat or drink, or how you treat your body, how will you control your thoughts or your words? In short, physical discipline builds spiritual discipline.

- **You Honor God by Taking Care of Your Temple.** As we discussed in this Mission's Introduction, your body isn't just yours—it belongs to God. Taking care of it shows you respect what He's given you.

Mission Objective: Complete one physical challenge today that pushes you beyond your normal effort—whether that's five more reps, a longer walk, or trying something new.

MISSION PLAN

Pick a physical challenge that stretches you beyond what's comfortable. This can be something that fits within your normal workout routine. But make sure you do more than you normally do. Here are some quick examples of what this might look like for you. Whatever it is, remember to modify this mission so that it matches your health and current fitness level.

If You Already Work Out:

- Add 5 more reps to one or all of your sets.
- Go heavier than usual on one exercise.
- Run an extra quarter mile.

- Hold your plank position 15 seconds longer than you normally would.

If You Don't Work Out Regularly:

- Do 10 push-ups (rest between reps if needed).
- Do 20 squats.
- Take a 15-minute walk.
- Do a 60-second wall sit.

Cardio Options:

- Run, jog, or walk faster than your normal pace.
- Bike or row for distance.
- Jump rope for 3 minutes.
- Take the stairs instead of the elevator all day.

Level Up:

- Listen to worship music while you work out.
- Pray while you walk or run.
- Thank God for the strength He's given you with every rep.

Whatever you choose, don't quit when it gets difficult. That's where the growth happens. Push past the moment you want to stop. That's where you build real strength.

MISSION TOOLS

- **Your Body**. No gym membership needed. Push-ups, squats, lunges, and planks require zero equipment.

- **Workout Space**. A room, a park, a driveway, or a gym—wherever you can exercise.
- **A Timer**. Use your phone to track your time or count your reps.
- **Water**. To stay hydrated before, during, and after your workout.
- **The Right Mindset**. Remember, you're not just building your body—you're honoring God.

ESTIMATED COMPLETION TIME

1 to 20 minutes

Depending on how long you want to exercise.

MISSION FUEL

Everyone who competes in the games goes into strict training. They do it to get a crown that will not last, but we do it to get a crown that will last forever.
—1 Corinthians 9:25

No discipline seems pleasant at the time, but painful. Later on, however, it produces a harvest of righteousness and peace for those who have been trained by it. **—Hebrews 12:11**

"The resistance that you fight physically in the gym and the resistance that you fight in life can only build a strong character." —Arnold Schwarzenegger

Practical Nutrition Tip: Your body is a machine—fuel it like one. Before you train, eat something with protein and carbs: a couple of eggs, a protein bar, or some oatmeal with berries and nuts. After you're done, don't skip the recovery meal. Steak and potatoes, chicken and rice, or a protein shake—real food that rebuilds what you just tore down. Skip the junk food, but don't be afraid to eat like a man who just did some real work.

The truth is: Every time you choose to strengthen your body, you're honoring the One who gave it to you. So, don't quit when it gets tough. Dig deep. Push through. That's where the growth happens. You've got this.

Now go—armor up, get strong, and honor God with your body!

MISSION DEBRIEF

Now that you've completed this mission, take some time to reflect on these questions:

1. What physical challenge did you complete?

2. How did it feel to push yourself beyond your normal effort?

3. Did you want to quit? What kept you going?

4. On a scale of 1 to 10 (10 being the most), how challenging was this?

5. What did you learn about your physical strength? About your mental toughness?

6. How did honoring God with your body change your perspective on fitness?

7. What will you do differently next time?

8. How can physical strength help you be a better man?

MISSION 8

GO DARK

Silence is the ultimate weapon of power.
—Charles de Gaulle

When's the last time you went a full day without checking your phone, turning on the TV, or scrolling through social media? For most of us, the answer is never. We've become so wired to digital noise that we don't realize how much it's draining us—mentally, spiritually, and emotionally. But that ends today!

The title of this mission, Go Dark, is a term that originates from military operations. When a unit 'goes dark', they cut all communications to avoid detection. No signals. No transmissions. Complete radio silence. It's the perfect term for what you're about to do: silence the noise in your life—or what I call *Cut Through the Noise*.

Today, you're going dark— cutting off the digital noise so God can restore your soul. Think of it as a digital fast.

But before you continue, understand that you're in an all-out war for your attention. Every time you unlock your phone, turn on the radio, watch your favorite sports team, or check your social media feed, someone is fighting for your attention. Don't believe me? Drive down the road for ten minutes and count how many billboards, bumper stickers, and business signs you see competing for your eyes.

I actually did this once on a forty-minute drive to my chiropractor. During that short trip, I counted over 400 advertisements. That's right—400. And that's just what I saw on the road. I'm not even talking about all the jingles and advertisements I heard on the radio. Now that's just a small snapshot of real life.

Digital marketers report that "people are exposed to more than 4,000 ads every day—up from just 500 in the 1970s." The point is: companies spend billions of dollars trying to capture your attention so you'll buy their products or services. They don't care if you're distracted, running on spiritual fumes, or missing quality time alone with God.

Furthermore, they won't tell you that *every* second you spend consuming their content is a second stolen from your life. From your family. From your calling. From your walk with God.

Remember the "Cease Fire" mission from Chapter 4? That mission is about pausing—being still long enough to hear

God's voice. This mission takes it further. It's about silencing the noise that pulls you away from His presence. Because "let's be honest—the noises aren't getting softer, they're getting LOUDER."

So why a full communications blackout?

Because God speaks in the quiet. Psalm 23 says He "restores my soul"—but how can He restore you if you never slow down long enough for Him to recharge your spirit? Seriously, take a few moments to think about that.

Does your life feel too busy or rushed right now?

It's no secret that we live in the most distracted generation in history. Studies reveal that "men spend an average of three hours a day watching TV. Over eighteen billion texts get sent every day. Google processes more than 63,000 searches per second. And the average person checks their phone over 100 times daily." Are you kidding me?

And here's the embarrassing part: goldfish have longer attention spans than we do. Goldfish—eight seconds. Humans—seven seconds. In that aspect, we're literally losing to fish. And it doesn't stop there.

We scroll before we pray. We idolize sports more than we worship God. We spend more time being entertained than engaging with the people who love us most.

Here's the brutal truth: Satan doesn't need you to sin to destroy you. He just needs to keep you distracted. If he can keep you focused on something else long enough, you'll forget or fail to spend quality time with God.

Today's mission: Go dark for 24 hours. No social media, no binge-watching, no mindless scrolling. Disconnect, unplug, cut the signal—whatever it takes—and let God restore your soul.

This isn't about punishing yourself or checking a box. It's about taking back control. About getting your life back in order. When you go dark, you make room for what *truly* matters—time with God, your loved ones, and yourself.

Distractions are one of the enemy's favorite weapons—and every man is a target. My book, *Cut Through the Noise: 4 Steps to Joy, Peace, and Freedom,* will help you get back your life and reconnect with God on a deeper level. But today, keep it simple and go dark for 24 hours.

MISSION PURPOSE

Mission: For the next 24 hours, cut out all forms of digital technology unless it's for emergency purposes. This includes social media, TV, YouTube, podcasts, video games, and any other non-essential entertainment.

Here's why: because your attention determines your direction.

- **Distraction is a Primary Weapon of the Enemy**. If Satan can't make you sin, he'll keep you busy and distracted. When your mind is always consumed by digital noise, you never make real progress in your faith or your life.

- **Clarity Comes in the Silence**. God's voice isn't found in the chaos of your feed. It's in the stillness. Go dark, and you'll start hearing Him more clearly.
- **Self-Control is a Force Multiplier**. If you can master your attention, you can master your life. Going dark builds the discipline you need for every other battle you'll face.
- **You'll Discover What You've Been Missing**. When you cut the signal, you'll realize how much life the noise has been stealing. Your mind will be clearer. Your relationships stronger. Your soul restored.

Mission Objective: Replace screen time with quality time with God, with your family, or with His creation so God *can restore* what your distractions *have been stealing* from you.

MISSION PLAN

For the next 24 hours, eliminate these:

- Social media (Instagram, Facebook, X, all of it)
- Streaming services (Netflix, Hulu, YouTube, etc.)
- Video games
- Radio and Podcasts (unless specifically for worship or Bible teaching)
- Internet and app usage
- Any other digital entertainment

Instead, replace all this noise with things that restore your soul. Here are some ideas:

Spend Real Time with God

- Read Scripture without distractions
- Pray without rushing—talk to the Lord like He's right there (because He is – Genesis 28:15)
- Journal what God is showing you
- Worship God with music that draws you closer

Be Fully Present with Your Loved Ones

- Put your phone in another room during meals
- Have a real conversation with your wife and kids
- Look them in the eye when they talk
- Be there fully engaged—not just physically, but mentally and emotionally

Experience God's Creation

- Go for a walk without headphones or earbuds and listen to the world God made
- Look up at the night sky to remind yourself how big and powerful God is
- Sit outside and just breathe

MISSION TOOLS

Here are a few suggestions:

- **A Bible** (a physical copy instead of an app).

- **A journal.**
- **A physical book**. If you need additional help, try my book, *Cut Through the Noise*. It's a tactical guide for eliminating hurry and reconnecting with God in four easy-to-follow steps. You can learn more at: JeffJerina.com / Books / Cut-Through-the-Noise
- **A watch.** So you're not tempted to check your phone for the time
- **Mental discipline.** Fasting from all digital technology for 24 hours will test your self-control. But don't give in. Stay the course. You can do it!

ESTIMATED COMPLETION TIME

24 hours.

A total digital blackout—one full day off the grid. Shut down the screens, silence the feeds, and disengage from all the noise. Use this time to recharge your soul.

MISSION FUEL

But seek first his kingdom and his righteousness, and all these things will be given to you as well.
—Matthew 6:33

Set your hearts on things above, not on earthly things.
—Colossians 3:2

He makes me lie down in green pastures, he leads me beside quiet waters, he restores my soul.
—Psalm 23:2-3

"The more we are distracted by earthly things, the less we are attracted to eternal truths." —Jeff Jerina

The more we are distracted by earthly things, the less we are attracted to eternal truths.

"Don't settle for a life that's distracted by the world. Instead, experience the freedom of a life that's devoted to God." —Jeff Jerina

Tactical Tip: The first few hours of this mission will be tough because your brain has been hardwired for noise. When the urge hits to grab your phone, turn on the TV, or fill the silence with distractions, **don't take the bait.** Do something different instead. Take a walk. Do some push-ups. Open your Bible. Pray. Anything that breaks the pattern.

Because every minute you take back is a minute God can use to restore what the noise has been stealing.

Go dark.

You can do it.

MISSION DEBRIEF

Reflect on what you learned and how you grew from this operation:

1. How did it feel to go a full day off the grid?

2. What did you notice about your thoughts, emotions, or focus during the fast?

3. Did you feel closer to God? Why or why not?

4. On a scale of 1 to 10 (10 being the hardest), how tough was this mission?

5. What was your biggest temptation to break radio silence?

6. What did you do instead of checking your phone or getting online? How did it feel?

7. How did this mission impact you or someone else?

8. What will you do differently next time? *Make this a regular practice or extend it longer?*

MISSION 9

SHARPEN YOUR EDGE

Once you stop learning, you start dying.
—Albert Einstein

A dull blade is useless in battle.
It doesn't matter how strong the steel was when it was forged or how many victories it's seen. Once it loses its edge, its effectiveness is compromised.

The same is true for you.
When you stop sharpening yourself—your mind, your body, your skills—you lose your edge. Your focus drifts. Your confidence fades. Your strength weakens. Before long, you go from thriving to merely surviving.

And here's the brutal truth: most men don't even realize it's happening until it's too late. They drift through life, barely getting through the day, instead of getting something from it and making it count.

That drift isn't just habit or laziness—it's conditioning. We've trained ourselves to avoid pain at all costs. To choose comfort and take the easy road whenever possible. Maybe it's watching sports instead of reading Scripture. Maybe it's grabbing fast food instead of cooking a healthy meal. Or perhaps it's staying late at work instead of having that difficult conversation with your wife. Do that long enough, and your mind automatically chooses the path of least resistance every time.

But you can break that pattern. God designed your mind to grow stronger through use. Every time you learn something new, your brain fires fresh neural connections. Stop learning, and those pathways weaken. "Use it or lose it" isn't just a saying—it's a neurological fact.

Here's the good news: there's never been a better time to sharpen your edge. Almost any skill or information you need is a click away. All you have to do is search for it online. I've learned to fix my car, repair my house, and tackle difficult challenges—all from watching free YouTube videos. The knowledge is out there. You just have to use it.

Just like the biblical account of David. Every day he tended sheep, he had to stay sharp—because danger could strike at any moment. Lions. Bears. Threats from every direction. Each one forced him to think fast and act decisively. Every challenge honed his skills and strengthened his spirit. By the time he faced Goliath, he wasn't just ready—he was unstoppable. His daily preparation had equipped him for battle.

James Allen said it best: "Men are anxious to improve their circumstances but are unwilling to improve themselves; they therefore remain bound." Ouch! That hits hard—but I know the feeling. Maybe it's because we all want more—a better job, a stronger marriage, a deeper faith. But we skip the one thing that makes it all possible: sharpening ourselves first.

God didn't design you to coast. He created you to grow. Proverbs 1:5 says, "Let the wise hear and increase in learning." In other words, wisdom grows through action—your action. And don't miss this: you can't sharpen anyone else if you've gone dull yourself. So, let's fix that today!

God didn't design you to coast. He created you to grow.

Do something in the next 24 hours that makes you sharper—mentally, physically, or spiritually.

Take a small step, but make it count. Learn a new skill. Read a passage that challenges you. Study a principle that stretches your thinking. Every intentional effort hones your edge and prepares you for the battles ahead.

Whatever it is, do something today that makes you better than you were yesterday. Because God doesn't just call leaders—He shapes them. And that shaping happens one day, one lesson, one choice at a time.

MISSION PURPOSE

Mission: Sharpen your edge today—mentally, physically, or spiritually.

The goal of this mission is simple: take one intentional step that sharpens you and helps you perform better in everyday life. And remember: your mind works like a muscle—challenge it, and it grows stronger. Ignore it, and it weakens. There's no middle ground or static condition.

- **Stagnation kills effectiveness.** When growth stops, performance plateaus. Skills dull without use, and progress slows without challenge.
- **Sharp men adapt under pressure.** Life will throw you curveballs—some expected, some not. A sharp or trained mind adjusts and responds. A dull or untrained mind only reacts.
- **You're either growing or dying.** Spiritually, mentally, physically—nothing stays the same. If you're not *intentionally* getting better, you're *automatically* getting worse. Without intentional effort, decline becomes the default.

Your mission today: Spend 15–30 minutes learning something new—something that sharpens your mind, strengthens your body, or deepens your faith. If the activity hits all three, even better.

As you execute this mission, think of each small step as another strike on your blade. Every page you read, every skill you practice, every challenge you tackle hones your mind, your spirit, and your abilities. Growth isn't a one-time event—it's a lifelong commitment.

Mission Objective: Strengthen your mind, body, or spirit by learning or practicing something new. Each day you do this, you build habits and skills that help you grow, stay sharp, and handle life's challenges better.

MISSION PLAN

Pick one of these areas to sharpen today—and be intentional about it. Don't just go through the motions; stay focused and engaged on the task at hand.

Sharpen Your Faith

- Dive into a Bible topic you've always wondered about—grace, spiritual warfare, or creation.
- Explore the historical context of a story you know.
- Dig into the life of a biblical figure like David, Paul, or Daniel—see what made them unshakeable.
- Memorize a verse that speaks directly to your life.

Sharpen Your Mind

- Tackle a practical skill you've been avoiding—basic investing, time management, or home repair.

- Read a chapter or blog post on leadership or personal growth—think of it as tactical intelligence.
- Watch a documentary about something you're curious about.
- Study a topic related to your work or hobby.

Sharpen Your Body

- Learn the proper form for an exercise you've been doing wrong.
- Study nutrition—to better understand what your body actually needs.
- Try a new workout technique or training method.
- Learn basic first aid or CPR.

Sharpen Your Skills

- Fix something around your house.
- Master a cooking technique.
- Practice a communication skill—listening, giving honest feedback, or handling tough conversations.
- Learn something your kids are into so you can connect on their level.
- Pick up a fun skill—like a card trick, juggling, or a musical instrument. This will challenge you and spark creativity.

Lock It In

- Write down the key takeaway from what you learned.

- Teach it to someone else—if you can teach it, you own it.
- Apply it immediately—even in a small way. Action solidifies learning.

Bottom line: This mission isn't about becoming an expert in a single day. It's about being sharper than you were yesterday. Treat each page read, skill practiced, and challenge tackled as a strike on your blade. Growth is a daily operation—commit to it.

MISSION TOOLS

Here are a few simple tools you already have access to—no special equipment required:

- **A Bible.** Dig into a new passage, topic, or truth and let it sharpen your thinking.
- **A Book**. Pick one that stretches you and helps you grow in some way.
- **The Internet.** Tutorials, documentaries, and courses put world-class learning at your fingertips—if you use it to grow, not scroll.
- **A Podcast, Sermon, or Bible commentary**. Gain wisdom from experienced teachers.
- **A Mentor**. Learn from someone who's already walked the road you're on right now.
- **A Journal**. Write down what you learn so it sticks.
- **Your hands**. Learn by doing—build something, fix something, or try something new.

ESTIMATED COMPLETION TIME

15 to 30 minutes.

That's all the time you need—or take as long as it takes. The goal isn't a one-time task; it's about building a healthy habit you can practice throughout your lifetime.

MISSION FUEL

As iron sharpens iron, one man sharpens another.
—Proverbs 27:17

If the ax is dull, and one does not sharpen the edge, then he must use more strength; but wisdom brings success.
—Ecclesiastes 10:10

"Formal education will make you a living; self-education will make you a fortune." —Jim Rohn

Here's the deal: every day, you're either getting sharper or duller. Stronger or weaker. Moving forward or falling back. There's no neutral ground. You're either growing or dying.

Look at Edmond Dantès in *The Count of Monte Cristo*. He was thrown into the worst prison imaginable—for a crime he didn't commit. His future was stolen. His life was buried behind stone walls. He could've quit, accepted defeat. But he didn't.

He turned his prison cell into a classroom.

He studied. He trained. He improved. Year after year, he sharpened his edge. When he finally escaped, he wasn't just free—he was unstoppable.

A simple sailor became a man no one could beat.

Why?

Because he refused to waste a single day.

That's your move today.

Not perfection, but **intentional action.**
One step that makes you sharper than you were yesterday.

Take the mission.

Sharpen your edge.

Step forward now.

MISSION DEBRIEF

After completing the mission, take a moment to reflect:

1. What did you learn today?

2. How will this new knowledge strengthen your faith, skills, or daily life?

3. Where did you feel resistance—mental, emotional, or spiritual—and how did you push through it?

4. On a scale of 1 to 10, (10 being the toughest) how challenging was this mission?

5. What did this mission reveal about yourself? About God?

6. How did this mission impact you or someone else?

7. What's your next step? *Go deeper, pick a harder challenge, or immediately apply what you learned?*

MISSION 10

EMBRACE DISCOMFORT

Do not pray for easy lives. Pray to be stronger men.
—John F. Kennedy

No pain, no gain.

You've heard it before—screamed by a coach in practice, said by your dad when you wanted to quit, or thrown at you by a buddy pushing you to lift more at the gym. Those words stuck because deep down, you knew they were true.

But somewhere along the way, we stopped living by them. We hit snooze when we should get up. We scroll when we should pray. We say, "I'll do it tomorrow," when we know it needs to happen today.

Comfort became the norm—our default setting.
And as nice as it feels, comfort doesn't build strong men.
It creates soft ones.

Here's the part nobody wants to admit: Every man loves the *idea* of strength... until he sees what it actually costs.

Because strength isn't formed with ease.

It's forged under pressure.

Under resistance.

Under hard work.

Under discomfort.

Ask any soldier. They don't train for convenience—they train for war. They push through tired legs, sore muscles, and cold mornings—not because it *feels* good, but because it *builds* something good: grit, discipline, and readiness.

God gives us the same charge:

> *Endure hardship as a good soldier of Christ Jesus.*
> **—2 Timothy 2:3**

Meaning: lean in when it gets hard.

Here's what I've learned: every time you choose the easy road—the path of least resistance—you get weaker. More comfortable with being comfortable. But every time you pick the hard thing, you get stronger. And over time, those tough choices shape you into the man God created you to be. Not a perfect man—but a disciplined one. A man who shows up. A man who doesn't quit. A man who faces his battles head-on. A man with resolve. A man who leads.

Today's mission: Do one hard thing on purpose.

Wake up when you don't want to.
Pray when you'd rather scroll.
Open your Bible before you check your phone.
Have that tough conversation you've been avoiding.
Choose the workout over the couch.
Choose discipline over delay.

Pick something uncomfortable and do it.

Because growth never happens in comfort. It happens when you push past what's easy.

Growth never happens in comfort. It happens when you push past what's easy.

MISSION PURPOSE

Mission: Do something difficult today.

Somewhere along the line, we bought the lie that says: Avoid pain. Take it easy. Stay comfortable. Play it safe. Get instant results.

But that's not how warriors are built.

That's not how disciples are formed.

Read the gospels. Study the early disciples in Acts. Their path was filled with hardship—trials, struggles, tough choices, challenging actions, and persecution. Some even faced death. Real growth—the kind that transforms you from the inside out—only happens when you push past what's easy. When you go beyond your limits.

Today, you're going to choose discomfort over ease. You're going to do something hard on purpose. Not to punish yourself, but to strengthen yourself.

Because discipline is what separates men who *talk about* change from men who *actually* change.

Here's what's on the line: Comfort kills growth.

- **Growth Happens Under Pressure**. Muscles don't grow from easy workouts. Character isn't built from easy choices. If you never face challenges, you'll never get stronger.
- **Discipline Creates Freedom**. When you can control yourself, your circumstances can't control you. You're no longer at the mercy of your cravings, temptations, or whatever life throws at you.
- **Hard Things Build Grit**. Life hits hard. Real hard. A man who's trained himself to handle discomfort doesn't crumble when things get tough.
- **Jesus Embraced Discomfort**. The Son of God, our Commander-in-Chief, endured pain, rejection, and

the cross. If He chose the hard road for our sake, why do we keep looking for the easy one?

Mission Objective: Build your character, sharpen your discipline, and grow stronger by refusing the easy path.

MISSION PLAN

Pick one way to push past your comfort zone.

- **Physically.** Choose the harder workout on purpose. Add weight. Do more reps. Run an extra mile. Don't tap out when your mind says "enough."
- **Mentally.** Face a fear. Take responsibility. Have that difficult conversation. Or tackle something you've been avoiding.
- **Spiritually.** Say no to comfort for a day. Wake up earlier to pray. Dive deeper into Scripture. Or fast from something that's been controlling you.

The goal of this mission is to help you:

- Build discipline
- Strengthen your will
- Train yourself to choose progress over comfort

MISSION TOOLS

- **A Challenge.** Pick something that pushes you beyond your limits.

- **The Proper Mindset**. Get comfortable being uncomfortable.
- **A reminder**. Write down *'Discipline Over Comfort'* where you'll see it regularly.
- **Your Bible**. Find a verse that fuels you.

ESTIMATED COMPLETION TIME

10 to 30 minutes.

Remember, it's not about the time it takes, but the effort you give.

MISSION FUEL

Endure hardship as discipline; God is treating you as His children.
—Hebrews 12:7

Weak men avoid discomfort. Strong men embrace it.

Choose discipline over ease.

Stay the course.

MISSION DEBRIEF

After completing the mission, take a moment to reflect:

1. What challenge did you take on today?

2. How did it feel to push past your comfort zone?

3. Did you have a moment when you wanted to quit? What did you do instead?

4. On a scale of 1 to 10 (10 being the hardest), how challenging was this mission?

5. Where do you sense God stretching or shaping you through this experience?

6. How did this mission affect your mindset, attitude, or confidence?

7. What's one area of your life where you now feel more prepared to handle discomfort or difficulty?

SECTION III

MULTIPLY YOUR IMPACT

MISSION 11

DEPLOY GENEROSITY

We make a living by what we get,
but we make a life by what we give.
—Winston Churchill

Have you ever noticed how some guys panic every time an unexpected expense hits?

A flat tire becomes a crisis.
A small home repair turns into a month-long disaster.

Meanwhile, other men take the same hits and barely flinch.

It's easy to assume the difference is their income. But it isn't.

If you're like me, you've known guys who make great money but never stop worrying about their finances, and others with far less who seem bulletproof when life throws a punch.

I knew someone like that—he worked for me part-time. No matter his job, he struggled to make ends meet. His truck was always breaking down. His bills came in bigger and faster than his paychecks.

Yet he was the happiest guy I knew.

Whatever life threw at him, he never blinked. Instead, he'd smile and start singing this little song he made up: "Thank you, Jesus. Thank you, Jesus. Thank you, Jesus—right now."

This man understood something about contentment that most of us are still trying to figure out.

What's the secret? What causes some men to be unshakable while others live in constant worry about what might go wrong next?

It comes down to this: you can tell a lot about a man by how tightly he holds onto what he has.

Think about a poker game. The nervous players clutch their cards tight, sweat when it's time to bet, and fold at the first sign of pressure. But the confident ones? Nothing seems to rattle them. They hold their cards loose, make calculated moves, and aren't afraid to go 'all in' when the moment is right.

That's exactly how life works. The same situation that crushes one man barely affects another, and it all depends on their grip.

So, if you'll allow me, I would like to ask you two questions.

1. Are you holding onto your money, time, and resources with clenched fists?
2. Or are you confident enough in God's provision to keep your hands open?

The world tells you to hoard your resources, guard your time, and look out for yourself, no matter what. Build a bigger savings account. Work more hours. Keep what you have because you might need it later.

The world's message is simple: there's never enough, so grab what you can and hold on tight.

But God's economy works differently. Proverbs 11:24 states:

> *One person gives freely, yet gains even more;*
> *another withholds unduly, but comes to poverty.*

In God's economy, the tighter you grip what you have, the more it slips through your fingers. But when you loosen your grip and trust Him, He takes care of what you actually need.

Here's what I've learned and still struggle with today: the tighter I grip, the more anxious I become. The more I try to control everything, the more out of control I really am. Trust me, I've been the guy lying awake at night doing mental math on bills, stressing over every expense, wondering if there would be enough to make it through the month. I've felt that knot in my stomach when an unexpected bill shows up. And I've made decisions based on fear instead of faith.

It wasn't until I started giving—not just my money, but my time and my talents—that I began to feel at peace. That's when I realized generosity isn't about having extra—it's about trust. It's choosing to believe that your Heavenly Father—who owns everything—will take care of you as you take care of others.

Today's mission is about taking a step of faith—loosening your grip on something you've been holding too tightly and watching what God does when you trust Him completely.

MISSION PURPOSE

Mission: Find one way to be generous today.

As you prepare for this mission, here are some quick thoughts on why this Spec Ops matters.

- **Giving breaks the grip of fear.** The enemy wants you to believe you don't have enough and that you never will. When you give generously, you're making a declaration that your trust *is* in God's provision, *not* your paycheck. Every act of generosity is an act of rebellion against the lie of scarcity.

Every act of generosity is an act of rebellion against the lie of scarcity.

- **It strengthens your faith muscles.** It's no secret that your faith grows when it's exercised. When you give sacrificially and watch God provide, your confidence in Him increases. You start to see His faithfulness in ways you never noticed before. What seemed impossible becomes possible when you're operating in His economy instead of the world's.

- **It reflects the heart of Christ.** Jesus gave everything for us—His comfort, His safety, His very life (see 1 Corinthians 15:1-4). When you give generously, you're showing the world what God's love looks like in action. You become His hands and feet to people who need to experience His goodness and presence.

- **It changes your perspective from scarcity to abundance.** Generous people don't worry about running out because they've learned that God's resources are endless. When you start giving, you start noticing how much you already have. Gratitude replaces anxiety. Contentment replaces the constant need for more.

Mission Objective: Give radically today. Whether it's your money, your time, or your talents, this act will require you to trust God's provision over your own ability to provide.

MISSION PLAN

Choose Your Method of Generosity

- **Give Financially**. You could donate to your church or a worthy cause, bless a struggling family, pay for someone's groceries, or cover a meal without that person knowing. The amount that you spend matters less than the faith it requires.
- **Give Your Time**. Help someone move, serve at your church, mentor a younger man, visit someone who's lonely, or volunteer for a cause you care about. Time is more valuable than money.
- **Share Your Skills**. Use what you're good at to help someone else. Fix something for a neighbor, help with someone's budget, teach a skill, or use your professional expertise to serve someone else.

Execute Your Plan

- Pick one of the methods above.
- Identify who you're going to bless.
- Act on it today—don't wait.
- Give with no expectation of getting anything back.
- Pay attention to how God moves in your heart.

MISSION TOOLS

- **Your finances**. Be ready to give—even when it feels uncomfortable or inconvenient.
- **Your time**. Show up for someone who needs you.
- **Your unique skills and abilities**. Whatever God made you good at, use it to serve others.
- **Your heart**. Stay willing and open to God's leading—because generosity isn't about what you have, but trusting Him with what you give.

ESTIMATED COMPLETION TIME

1 to 10 minutes.

Although this single act of generosity can take less than ten minutes of your time, the impact can last a lifetime—both for you and the person you bless.

MISSION FUEL

For where your treasure is, there your heart will be also.
—Matthew 6:21

Give, and it will be given to you: good measure, pressed down, shaken together, and running over, will be put into your lap. For with the same measure that you use, it will be measured back to you.
—Luke 6:38

It is more blessed to give than to receive.
—Acts 20:35

Let each one give as he purposes in his heart, not grudgingly or of necessity; for God loves a cheerful giver.
—2 Corinthians 9:7

Let them do good, that they be rich in good works, ready to give, willing to share.
—1 Timothy 6:18

Remember: Giving isn't a loss—it's an investment in God's kingdom. When you trust the Lord completely, you discover just how fully He can be trusted. Every act of generosity is a step deeper into the abundant life He has for you.

Now go—give boldly.

Trust completely.

Watch how God moves!

MISSION DEBRIEF

Once you've completed the mission, debrief with these questions:

1. What did you give today?

2. How did it feel to give with no strings attached?

3. Did you struggle with letting go? Why or why not?

4. On a scale of 1 to 10 (10 being the hardest), how hard was this mission?

5. What did you learn about yourself? About God?

6. How did this mission impact you or someone else?

7. What will you do differently next time? *Give more often? Trust God in bigger ways? Be more intentional?*

MISSION 12

INVEST IN WHAT MATTERS

Man has two supreme loyalties—to country and to family. With most men, the second is the stronger.
— Captain Sir Basil Liddell Hart

You can win at work and still lose at home.

Not because you're lazy. Not because you don't care. But because somewhere along the way, you started fighting the wrong battles.

You climbed the ladder. Built a career. Brought home the paycheck. Did everything you thought you were supposed to do. And then one day, you slowed down long enough to notice—something's off.

Your wife seems distant. Your kids are practically grown. And the family you worked so hard to provide for feels strangely unfamiliar.

The crazy part? This doesn't happen because you're a bad man. It happens because your focus—without warning—shifts in the wrong direction.

Your work demands more.

Stress piles higher.

The urgent drowns out the important.

And slowly, quietly, the people who matter most get what's *left* of you instead of the *best* of you.

Maybe you've built a solid career. Maybe your bank account looks healthy. Maybe you've earned respect at the office. But if you're giving scraps at home, you're still bankrupt where it counts. You gave your loved ones everything except what they actually need most: YOU.

Here's the reality: your kids won't remember your job title. They'll remember whether you showed up. Your wife won't brag about your salary. She'll remember if you made her feel loved and spent time with her.

The world keeps pushing the same message: grind harder, chase bigger, and hustle more. Sure, hard work matters. But too many men get trapped winning everywhere except the place that matters most—home.

Somewhere along the way, success got redefined. And most of us never stopped to question it.

But as a warrior for Christ, you must know that God didn't design you to just provide financially. He called you to lead, love, and invest deeply in the people He placed under your care.

And make no mistake—Scripture doesn't let us hide behind good intentions or busy schedules.

> *But if anyone does not provide for his own, and especially for those of his household, he has denied the faith and is worse than an unbeliever.*
> **—1 Timothy 5:8**

Read that again.

This verse isn't just about money. It's about total provision—spiritual, emotional, and relational. Meaning:

- Your presence.
- Your leadership.
- Your time.

These are the real investments.

This isn't theory or some new-age thought. It's real life.

Seriously, when your life is over, your job won't be standing at your bedside. Your house won't be holding your hand. Your bank account won't be telling your stories.

It's the people you invested in that will be there.

Or they won't.

And that decision is being made right now—in the small moments you either show up for or let slip away.

Today's mission: Spend intentional time with someone you love.

Not distracted time. Not disengaged time. Real-time. The kind where you abandon your agenda, turn off your phone, and be fully engaged in their presence, actually listening to and spending time with them.

Because strong men don't just build careers. They build families. And that starts with being fully present and fully engaged.

If you need a quick reminder of what this looks or the benefits of investing your life where it matters most, listen to one of these episodes I recorded on my podcast:

- *The Power of Being Fully Present with Your Kids—Why Your Engagement is Their Superpower*

  Link: JeffJerina.com/Podcast/Being-Fully-Present-with-Your-Kids

- *Christian Leadership and Parenting: How to Build a Legacy that Lasts*

  Link: JeffJerina.com/Podcast/How-to-Build-A-Lasting-Legacy-Christian-Leadership-Parenting

MISSION PURPOSE

Mission: Spend intentional time with someone you love.

Here's what's on the line: the strength, trust, and longevity of your relationships.

- **Your Family is Your First Mission**. Before you lead anyone else, you lead at home. If you're disconnected from your family, your foundation is already cracked. And a soldier who can't secure his base will never win the war. Simply put, strong families don't happen by accident.
- **Your Presence is Your Leadership**. Your wife needs your attention, not just your paycheck. Your kids need your example, not just your rules. The people closest to you don't need more words—they need your presence. And none of that happens if you're always somewhere else (not just physically but emotionally), even when you're technically "there."
- **Busyness is the Enemy of Connection**. Everyday life will try to steal your focus. That's why you always have to be on your guard—to continually fight for what matters. Nobody's going to hand you

more padding or margin in your life—you have to create it.

- **You'll Never Regret This Time**. You'll regret the deals you chased, the hours you gave away, and the idols you worshipped. But you'll never regret the time you spent with the people you love. That investment always pays off.

Mission Objective: Strengthen one key relationship today by showing up fully—so trust deepens, connection grows, and the people who matter most in your life feel seen, valued, and secure.

MISSION PLAN

Today's mission is about people, not productivity. So, choose one of these individuals to spend time with and show them you love them in some way. Here are a few examples on how to complete this mission:

For Your Wife

- Plan a simple date—go out for coffee or lunch, take a walk around the neighborhood, anything where you can talk.
- Write her a note telling her what you appreciate about her.
- Pray with her, not just for her.
- Ask her, "How are you doing?" "How's your heart?" and then actually listen.

For Your Kids

- Get on their level—play a game they love to play, play catch, or read a book together.
- Ask them about their day and listen undistracted to their whole answer.
- Turn off your phone, shut down your computer, and be fully there.
- Read a Bible story together before they go to bed.

For Your Parents or Siblings

- Call them up and ask how they're doing.
- Tell them something you're grateful to them for.
- If possible, visit them face-to-face.

For a Close Friend

- Check in on them and see how they're doing.
- Invite your friend for coffee or lunch and take this time to be fully present.
- Encourage them specifically about something you see in them.

Whoever you decide to invest in today and however you decide to show them value, please remember that this isn't about spending money. It's about spending yourself. Your attention. Your presence. Your time. That's what people actually need from you.

MISSION TOOLS

- **Your Full Attention**. Put your phone away. Turn off your notifications. Be all there, fully present, and fully engaged.

- **Conversation Starters**. Ask real questions: "How's your heart?" "What has God been teaching you?" "What's your biggest struggle right now?" "What can I do to support or encourage you better?"
- **Your Presence**. It's not about what you do in this mission. It's about who you're with and whether they feel seen and heard.
- **Follow Through**. If they mention something important, remember it or write it down, and follow up later. This small effort on your part makes a big impact. It shows them they're valued—that they matter to you.

ESTIMATED COMPLETION TIME

15 minutes to 1 hour

Not long. But long enough to show someone they matter.

MISSION FUEL

Teach us to number our days, that we may gain a heart of wisdom.
—Psalm 90:12

Remember the Lord, who is great and awesome, and fight for your families, your sons and your daughters, your wives, and your homes.
—Nehemiah 4:14

Be very careful, then, how you live… making the most of every opportunity.
—Ephesians 5:15-16

Let's be honest—**you can't get back your time.**

Once it's spent, it's gone. No rewind. No do-overs.

You can make more money.
You can rebuild a career.
You can recover from failure.

But you can't reclaim the years you weren't present.

Time is the one resource that never replenishes.

Every man is given the same 24 hours a day. The difference between the man who *stood his post* and the one who *abandoned it* isn't talent or opportunity—it's how he chose to spend those hours.

That's why your time matters.

Because **what you invest in—and where you choose to fight—determines everything else.**

When Jerusalem was under threat, Nehemiah didn't lead from a distance. He stayed close. He stayed alert. He stayed engaged (see Nehemiah 4). He understood that **the mission fails when the watchman leaves his post.**

The same is true for you.

The people God has placed under your care don't need promises about *someday*. They need your presence *today*.

Here's what separates good men from great ones: strong men don't just provide cover from afar—they continually show up and stay engaged in the fight.

You can scale every mountain, earn every medal, and stack every win—but **if your family becomes collateral damage along the way,
the mission has failed.**

If your family becomes collateral damage along the way, the mission has failed.

Your assignment is clear: secure the home front first.

Your wife needs you.
Your kids need you.
And the people closest to you need the *best of you*—not what's *left of you* after everyone else has taken their cut.

So go—be present.

Stand your post.

Invest in what matters.

Lead the people God entrusted to you.

MISSION DEBRIEF

After completing today's mission, reflect on these questions:

1. Who did you spend time with today? And how did you intentionally invest in their life?

2. How did they respond?

3. On a scale of 1 to 10 (10 being the most), how meaningful was this time together?

4. What distractions tried to pull you away? *Phone, work thoughts, stress, etc.*

5. What did this mission reveal about your priorities or what you truly value?

6. What did you learn about yourself? About them? About God?

7. What will you do differently in the future? *Be more consistent? Schedule it? Go deeper in conversations?*

MISSION 13

BUILD YOUR BROTHERHOOD

Courage is contagious. When a brave man takes a stand, the spines of others are stiffened.
—Billy Graham

A lone wolf is a dead wolf.

Maybe you've heard it—perhaps you've even wondered if that's you. The reality? Too many men try to go through life alone, thinking they have what it takes to handle it on their own. So, they suffer in silence, carry heavy burdens without support, and fight their battles with no backup.

But that's not how God designed you to live.

He created you for connection, for community, and for support—because no one is meant to fight life's battles alone.

> *As iron sharpens iron, so one man sharpens another.*
> **—Proverbs 27:17**

True strength doesn't come from isolation. It comes from walking shoulder to shoulder with other men.

This means that you need men who will stand beside you, pray for you, challenge you, and push you to be better. And whether you realize it or not—they need you, too.

The devil loves isolated soldiers. He picks them off one by one. A man fighting alone is easier to discourage, easier to tempt, and easier to take down. But a unit that fights together? That's a force he can't break.

Think about it. When's the last time you had a real conversation with another man?

Not surface-level talk about sports or work. I'm talking about the hard stuff—the things that make all of us as men feel a little weird and uncomfortable sharing. Things like your struggles, your doubts, and your fears. The mess you're dealing with that nobody else knows about.

When a man doesn't have that type of connection, he's isolated. He can be surrounded by others, but still feel completely alone in the fight. Whether it's a hidden sin, a strained marriage, or doubts about his faith—trying to handle it alone will break him down spiritually, mentally, and emotionally.

No matter how smart or strong you are, you can't fight your battles alone and expect to win. Even the toughest soldier can't hold the line by himself. You need brothers who will get in the mud with you—who will pray for you when you're down, who will call you out when you're drifting off course, and who will stand in the gap when the enemy attacks.

That's real brotherhood.

Not just guys you hang out with, but men you go to war with.

And here's the great news: you don't need an army. You only need a few good men. Maybe just one or two guys who will get in the foxhole with you. Men who've got your six—and know you've got theirs.

I'm grateful that I have friends like that. Guys who encourage me, pour into me, challenge me, and yeah—tell me things about myself that I don't always want to hear. Now, that's brotherhood.

That's what you're looking for. A small band of brothers you can count on when life hits hard.

And if you don't have it yet, today's mission is your first step toward building it.

Check in on another man.

Whether it's a brother-in-Christ, a friend, a mentor, or someone you haven't talked to in a while—reach out in some way. Send a text. Make a call. Grab a coffee.

That's how brotherhood is built.

MISSION PURPOSE

Mission: Check in on another man today.

You weren't made to fight alone. Ask anyone who's been in combat—the most dangerous place to be is separated from your unit.

Here's what's on the line: the strength and depth of your brotherhood.

- **Brotherhood Is Intentional**. Most guys know plenty of people. Coworkers. Neighbors. Guys from church. But how many have "brothers" they can actually count on? Men who know what's really going on in their lives. Not many. Brotherhood doesn't just happen. It's built through intentional connection—through checking in, showing up when it's inconvenient, letting another man know you care, and asking tough questions.
- **The Impact is Multiplied**. When you reach out to another man, you show him he doesn't have to carry his burdens alone. And when he does the same for you, you realize you don't either. You build him up, he builds you up. Think about how iron actually sharpens iron—two pieces of metal striking together,

sparks flying, friction building heat, raw force shaping both. That collision? That's real power. Real impact. And that's what forges both men into something stronger.

- **Jesus Lived This**. He didn't just teach His disciples from a distance. He walked with them. Ate with them. Suffered with them. Lived with them. Called them friends. That's the kind of brotherhood He's calling you to build.
- **Brotherhood Is Your Lifeline.** When you build a true brotherhood, you're not just strengthening other men. You're forging the network that will hold you up when you need it most.

Mission Objective: Strengthen one relationship today so you have brothers who truly know you and will stand with you when life gets tough.

MISSION PLAN

Take a few minutes today to connect with a good friend. Here's how you can complete this mission:

- **Call or Text**. Reach out and ask, "How's your walk with God? How can I pray for you?" Don't settle for surface-level "I'm fine" answers. Press in a little deeper.
- **Meet Up**. Grab coffee, go to lunch, hit the gym, or just spend time together. Face-to-face connection matters. There's something about sitting across from

another man that builds trust and opens conversation.

- **Pray for Him**. Whether he asks for it or not, cover him in prayer. If you're together, pray with him right there—don't wait or say I'll put you on my prayer list. If you can't meet, shoot up a prayer and let him know you did.

- **Be Real**. Share something personal. Ask deeper questions. Don't just talk about sports or work. Get to what's really going on in his life.

- **Offer Support**. If he's struggling, be there for him. Offer advice only when he asks for it. Hold him accountable if he needs it. Sit with him. Just listen. Yeah, I get it—listening without fixing goes against every instinct we have as men. But sometimes that's exactly what a brother needs: someone who hears him and reminds him that he's not alone in the fight. Sometimes the best thing you can do is show up and shut up.

MISSION TOOLS

- **Your phone**. Call, text, or message. Don't overthink it. Just reach out.

- **Your time**. Plan a meet-up or check in regularly. Put it on the calendar if you have to. Brotherhood doesn't happen by accident; it's proactive and purposeful.

- **A Willing Heart**. Be intentional. Show up. Be consistent. Your brothers need to know they can count on you.
- **Your Bible**. Share a verse if your friend needs encouragement. Point him back to God's truth when he's doubting or struggling.
- **The Special Ops Brotherhood Community**. Want to connect with other Christian men on mission? Join the Special Ops Brotherhood community where men are building real relationships, encouraging each other, and growing in faith together.

  Learn more at:

  JeffJerina.com / Books / SpecialOpsforMen / Resources

ESTIMATED COMPLETION TIME

1 to 10 minutes.

A simple check-in like this mission can change a man's day—or even his life.

MISSION FUEL

Carry each other's burdens, and in this way you will fulfill the law of Christ.
—Galatians 6:2

Two are better than one, because they have a good reward for their labor. For if they fall, one will lift up his companion…

—Ecclesiastes 4:9-10

Be devoted to one another in love, honor one another above yourselves.
—Romans 12:10 NIV

Therefore, encourage one another and build each other up, just as in fact you are doing.
—1 Thessalonians 5:11

There it is—straight from Scripture. Brotherhood isn't optional. It's essential.

The men around you need what you have to offer—your strength, your prayers, your friendship. And you need them too.

Don't wait for someone else to build your brotherhood. Start it yourself. Reach out first. Be the man who checks in, who shows up, who fights alongside his brothers instead of trying to go it alone.

A warrior without a brotherhood is an easy target.

Remember: A warrior without a brotherhood is an easy target. But a band of brothers on mission together? That's an unstoppable force.

Now move out—lock arms with your brothers, strengthen your unit, and never fight alone again.

MISSION DEBRIEF

After you've completed this mission, take a few minutes to reflect:

1. Who did you check in on today?

2. How did they respond?

3. What changed in your relationship because of this mission?

4. On a scale of 1 to 10 (10 being the hardest), how hard was this mission?

5. What did this mission reveal—about yourself, about him, about God's work in both of you?

6. What's your next step? *Make this a regular habit? Go deeper? Reach out to someone else?*

7. Who else in your life needs this kind of check-in?

MISSION 14

HONOR THE CALL

The only thing necessary for the triumph of evil is for good men to do nothing.
—Edmund Burke

What if you knew you'd been entrusted with something powerful enough to change someone's life forever? Not just make their day easier or fix a problem—but to alter their eternal destination.

Seriously—what if that was true?

If you had something like that— something with real, everlasting implications—would you use it? Would you share it freely? Or would you keep it to yourself, thinking you're not ready, not equipped, or strong enough to get the job done?

Here's the truth: you've *already* been entrusted with it.

As a soldier in Christ's army, you've been given a standing order—the Great Commission (Matthew 28:16-20). It's not a suggestion. It's a command. Jesus didn't issue this mandate to a select few or to the spiritually elite. He gave it to *every* believer. No exceptions. No excuses. Everyone.

Regardless of your age, education, background, or vocation—the moment you placed your faith in Jesus—you were commissioned. It wasn't optional. You don't need a title. You don't need a platform. You don't need permission. You don't even need to "feel ready." Because you've already been called.

> *For I am not ashamed of the gospel, because it is the power of God that brings salvation to everyone who believes.*
> **—Romans 1:16**

The gospel is the most powerful weapon ever placed in human hands. But unlike the weapons of this world, it doesn't destroy. It rescues. It redeems. It sets captives free.

And yet, too many men never deploy it. They remain silent. They keep it locked away, treating it like hidden treasure instead of a mission-critical message meant to be shared. Why?

Maybe it's fear of rejection. Maybe it's because you don't know where to start. Maybe you think you're not qualified enough. But here's what most men fail to realize: there is no greater honor you can give another human being than letting them know they are loved by God—and they don't need to do anything (now or in the future) to earn that love.

And the greatest way to show that love is to share the good news of Jesus Christ.

This mission isn't about having all the answers or memorizing the perfect evangelism script. It's not about being a theologian or knowing exactly what to say. God doesn't need polished messengers to complete His work.

Look at Moses—he wasn't gifted at speaking. How about Paul? He killed Christians before becoming an evangelist. The point is: God doesn't need perfect men. He needs obedient ones.

That's the heartbeat of this mission: honoring the call placed on your life and having the courage to step forward when the moment presents itself. And trust me—it will present itself.

To learn more about stepping forward when those divine moments present themselves or for deeper training on sharing your faith in a simple, natural way, check out my book and evangelism course *Faith Without Fear: How to Share What You Believe with Confidence and Power* at:

- JeffJerina.com/Books/FaithWithoutFear.

So, what does honoring the call look like in real life?

Warriors don't sit idle. They don't keep their training locked away. They stand ready to deploy what they've learned at a moment's notice. They don't stand silent while the battle rages. They move when they're called, even when their voice shakes and their hands tremble.

That's you. Right now.

You have something people desperately need—whether you realize it or not. Someone in your life today could be one conversation away from hearing about Jesus. One question away from opening their heart. One bold moment away from their eternity changing.

And you might be the only messenger they ever get.

Think about that. The only one.

Now, I know that may put some pressure on you. You might be thinking, *"C'mon, man—God is in control. He knows exactly what to do."* And you're right. He does. That's exactly why He drafted you in His army.

He chose you for this mission. Not because you're perfect, but because you're willing.

> *The harvest is plentiful but the workers are few.*
> **—Matthew 9:37**

Did you get that?

The need is *massive,* but the workers are few. In fact, research shows that 98% of Christians will never share their faith with anyone. Most will stay comfortable. Most will stay silent.

But you're not like most men.

You're one of the few. One of the proud. One of the brave who's ready to step up and honor the call today.

So, roll out. Share the gospel. And make disciples.

This is how you honor the call.

MISSION PURPOSE

Mission: Share the gospel or have a conversation about your Christian faith with at least one person today, honoring God's call and giving someone the greatest gift they could ever receive—the hope of Jesus Christ.

Here's what's on the line: someone's eternity.

That statement alone should be enough to execute this mission right now.

- **Faith Without Action Is Weak**. Well, actually, James said "dead" (James 2:17). But for this mission, in the context of sharing the gospel, we could say that 'silent faith' is a 'powerless faith'. When you share your faith, you're not just helping others—you're strengthening your personal walk with Christ. Every time you speak up, your confidence grows. Your faith deepens. Your relationship with God gets stronger.

- **You Could Be the Only Jesus Someone Sees**. Many people will never pick up a Bible. They may never step foot in a church. They may never seek God on their own. But they'll see you. They'll hear you. They'll see the difference God has made in your life as you share your testimony with them. Your presence is how they encounter Christ—through your story and through your life. You're the living, breathing messenger God has placed in their path.
- **Rejection Is Temporary—Eternity Is Forever**. Fear of sounding weird or feeling awkward is nothing compared to the eternal impact of leading someone to Christ. Yes, they might reject the message. They might think you're crazy. But what if they don't? What if this *one* conversation changes *everything* for them?
- **This Is Your Mandate as a Christian Soldier**. This isn't optional. It's a command from Jesus Himself (Mark 16:15). Men were made to lead. Lead someone to Jesus today.

Mission Objective: Grow bolder in sharing your faith while giving someone the opportunity to hear about the life-saving message of Jesus Christ, thereby honoring your call as a fisher of men (Matthew 4:19).

MISSION PLAN

This section gives you a quick, practical way to honor the call today. But if you want to go deeper—if you want to learn how to share your faith naturally, overcome the fear of sharing the gospel, and be truly equipped to lead others to Christ—that's exactly what my book and evangelism course *Faith Without Fear: How to Share What You Believe with Confidence and Power* were created for. You can check them out at: **JeffJerina.com/Books/FaithWithoutFear.**

But know this—the information I've outlined in this Mission Plan will help you be about the Master's business (Luke 2:49; John 15:15). Every conversation you have about Jesus expands His Kingdom. Every seed you plant matters for eternity.

And throughout my years of individual and group evangelism coaching, one of the most effective and easiest approaches I've witnessed is this: believers sharing their own personal story of salvation.

So let's start there.

SHARE YOUR STORY

The easiest and most powerful way to share the gospel is to tell someone how God has impacted your life (by sharing your testimony). Here's why—people relate to stories. Think about all those product reviews on Amazon. When you read one, you instantly connect with their experience about that product. Your salvation story is just that—your personal review of what Jesus has done in your life.

If you're a new believer—someone who recently placed their faith in Christ—here are some things to include when giving your testimony:

- What was your life like before you trusted in Jesus as your Lord and Savior?
- Who shared the gospel with you?
- How old were you when you trusted in Him?
- What happened when you gave your life to Him?
- What is your life like now?

If you're someone who's been a believer for a while—maybe someone more mature in their faith—share how Jesus is impacting your life right now:

- How is He changing you?
- What struggles is He helping you through?
- How has your relationship with Him grown?

No matter where you are in your Christian faith, your story is powerful because it's real. Nobody can argue with what God has done in your life.

SHARE A VERSE

If you want to go further, share a Bible verse. To help, you can memorize one of these or read one of them from your Bible or a Bible app. Here are some suggestions:

- For God so loved the world that he gave his one and only Son, that whoever believes in him shall not perish but have eternal life.
  —John 3:16
- For the wages of sin is death, but the gift of God is eternal life in Christ Jesus our Lord.
  —Romans 6:23

You don't need to complicate it.

Just point them to God's truth.

OTHER WAYS TO SHARE

- **Ask a Simple Question**. "Do you believe in God?", "Do you have any thoughts about faith?", or "Have you ever thought about eternity?" It sounds crazy, but a simple question like that can open the door to a life-changing conversation.
- **Offer to Pray for Someone**. If a coworker, friend, or family member is struggling, don't just say "I'll pray for you." Stop right there and pray with them. Out loud. In the moment. This way they know that there is at least one person who seriously cares for them. And that might be the interaction they need that prompts them to hear about Jesus.
- **Send a Message**. If talking in person feels too scary or hard right now, text someone a Bible verse, a link to a Christian podcast or video, or a word of encouragement.

The key here is to step out in boldness.

Remember: The opportunity is there—you just have to take it.

MISSION TOOLS

- **Your Testimony**. Your personal story is one of the most powerful tools you have. People can argue with theology, but they can't argue with what God has done in your life.

- **God's Word.** Keep John 3:16 or Romans 6:23 ready to share. Simple verses like this are packed with truth—God's truth.
- **A Willing Heart**. Pray for opportunities and the courage to take them. Ask God to open doors and give you the words to say.
- ***Faith Without Fear* Resources**. For deeper training on sharing your faith with confidence, check out my *Faith Without Fear* book and course at:

  Book:
  JeffJerina.com/Books/FaithWithoutFear

  Course:
  JeffJerina.com/Courses/ShareTheGospel

ESTIMATED COMPLETION TIME

1 to 10 minutes.

This mission is about seizing the moment. It could be a quick prayer, a short conversation, or a simple text. Don't overthink it—just act.

MISSION FUEL

Follow me, and I will make you fishers of men.
—Matthew 4:19

For God has not given us a spirit of fear, but of power and of love and of a sound mind.
—2 Timothy 1:7

How then will they call on him in whom they have not believed? And how are they to believe in him of whom they have never heard? And how are they to hear without someone preaching?
—Romans 10:14

But in your hearts revere Christ as Lord. Always be prepared to give an answer to everyone who asks you to give the reason for the hope that you have. But do this with gentleness and respect.
—1 Peter 3:15

Go into all the world and preach the gospel to every creature.
—Mark 16:15

Fear is not from God. Courage is.

The enemy wants you silent because he knows the power of the gospel. He knows that one conversation can destroy his hold on someone's life. He knows that your testimony and your boldness to proclaim the gospel can shatter the darkness.

So Satan whispers lies like: "They'll think you're weird." "You don't know enough." "It's not the right time." "They won't like you anymore." "Someone else will do it."

Don't believe the devil.

You don't need to be perfect. You don't need all the answers. You just need to be obedient.

Here's something that changed everything for me when I started sharing my faith—and I talk about this in detail in the *Faith Without Fear* training: your job isn't to save people. That's God's job—through the power of the Holy Spirit. **Your job is to simply be ready—to tell others about the life saving message of Jesus Christ.** Then leave the rest to God. You plant the seed. He grows it.

That takes the pressure off completely. Doesn't it? Because now you know that you're *not* responsible for the outcome—you're *only* responsible for your obedience.

There are your orders—directly from Scripture. Sharing the gospel isn't optional. It's mandatory.

We don't share Jesus because it's easy—we share Jesus because lives depend on it.

We don't share Jesus because it's easy—we share Jesus because lives depend on it.

Now roll out—step up, speak out, and honor the call today.

MISSION DEBRIEF

Here's your mission debrief. Before you go through it, remember that a successful outcome for this mission is not whether someone else places their faith in Jesus, but whether you were faithful in sharing the gospel.

1. Who did you talk to about Jesus today?

2. How did you start the conversation? *With your story, a verse, a question, prayer, or a message?*

3. How did they respond? *Were they encouraged, interested, indifferent, resistant, etc.?*

4. On a scale of 1 to 10 (10 being the hardest), how hard was this mission for you?

5. What fears or hesitations did you have? How did you overcome them?

6. Did you make any plans to follow up with the person you shared the gospel with? If so, what are they?

7. What will you do differently next time? *Be more direct? Share more of your story? Look for more opportunities?*

MISSION 15

PLOT YOUR COURSE

Set your course by the stars,
not by the lights of every passing ship.
—General Omar N. Bradley

A ship without a course is at the mercy of the current.

It doesn't matter how powerful the engine is or how skilled the crew may be. Without a clear heading, that ship goes wherever the wind and waves take it—and that's rarely where it was meant to go.

The same is true for your life.

If you drift long enough, you'll end up somewhere you never intended to be, doing something you never set out to do. It's what we call 'settling.'

Maybe you're there right now.

If so, you didn't veer off course because you lack motivation or aspirations. You drifted because nobody taught you how to plot your course.

No one showed you how to align your ambition with God's assignment.

So, like a lot of men, you move forward working hard, staying busy, juggling responsibilities—but without a precise heading. Yet, you're still clinging to hope that one day things will all come together.

And yes, although hope is powerful, it needs direction. That's what **this mission is about: direction.** A target you can aim your life at.

The other missions in this book strengthen you in specific areas—discipline, courage, health, leadership, mindset, faith, among others. This one makes sure that strength is aimed at the right target.

Because discipline without direction is wasted strength.

Discipline without direction is wasted strength.

It's the mission you return to after victories and setbacks, when you've accomplished what you set out to do, and when you sense God calling you higher.

Maybe you didn't drift intentionally. Maybe it happened gradually. Responsibilities increased. Expectations grew. Great opportunities came along. None of those seemed wrong at the time. But over months or even years, those small shifts added up. A delay here. A compromise there. A season of distraction that quietly stretched longer than it should have.

And before you realized it, the vision you once had for your life—your dreams, your goals, your plans—didn't seem as clear anymore.

Here's the reality: if you don't set your own course, someone—or something else—will set it for you.

And that path rarely leads where you want to go. It pulls you toward what's *urgent* instead of what's *important*. Toward what's *comfortable* instead of what's *calling*. Toward the *temporal* instead of the *eternal*. And quietly, without you even noticing, it will reshape the legacy you were called to leave.

In the military, being off course isn't a minor inconvenience—it's mission failure. Navigators don't guess. Pilots don't drift. Special operators don't wander. They're dialed in. They plot their route with precision, monitor it constantly, and course correct immediately when something pushes them off track. Even a one-degree error, sustained over time, can result in missing the objective entirely.

That's how we should approach our lives. Not casually or reactively. But intentionally.

Now, this isn't about chasing applause or accumulating possessions. It's about stewardship. When the Lord calls you home, you want to hear, "Well done, good and faithful servant" (Matthew 25:21). You want to know you used what He entrusted to you as best you could. That you aimed your life toward something, not just casually lived it.

Planning your life this way doesn't replace your faith—it expresses it.

> *Seek first the kingdom of God and His righteousness, and all these things will be added to you.* **—Matthew 6:33**

This mission isn't about building your kingdom and asking God to bless it. It's about seeking His kingdom first—and building your plans around that. And part of those plans needs to include others—how you'll serve, lead, and point people to Christ. A mission that benefits only you is too small.

Every decision you make is moving you somewhere.

The question is: are you choosing the destination and the impact you'll leave?

Stop drifting. Start directing.

Today's mission: Seek the Lord. Define your heading. Plot your course.

MISSION PURPOSE

Mission: Take action on plotting the course God has for your life.

Here's what's on the line: the life you were meant to live.

- **A Drifting Man Goes Nowhere.** Without a clear course, you drift. You get pushed off track by distractions, by other people's agendas, by the daily grind. A man without goals is like a soldier without a mission—present but purposeless. You were made for more than that.
- **The Future Rewards Men Who Plan for It**. Goals aren't just wishes. They're declarations of intent. When you write down where you want to go and what you want to do with your life, you're telling God, yourself, and the enemy: I know where I'm headed, and that's where I'm going. That kind of clarity creates momentum that no army can stop.
- **Small Wins Build Big Momentum**. You don't have to accomplish everything at once. Every goal you complete—no matter how small—is a victory worth celebrating. Each one builds the confidence and momentum to tackle the next. This is how transformation happens: one step, one win, one goal at a time.
- **Your Legacy Starts Now**. The decisions you make today determine the impact and legacy you leave tomorrow. Not just for your kids—but for their kids. Every goal you pursue, every dream you chase,

every promise you keep is a deposit into a legacy that outlasts you.

- **God Has a Plan—And So Should You**. Proverbs 16:9 says, "In their hearts humans plan their course, and the Lord establishes their steps." God expects you to plan. But here's the kicker, He asks you to hold it loosely and trust Him with the outcome.

Mission Objective: Create a clear, written vision for your life by setting goals for the next year, three years, and ten years—so you can stop drifting and start moving with purpose toward the life God designed for you.

MISSION PLAN

Here's your plan of attack. But before you write a single goal, do this first:

STEP 1: START WITH PRAYER

Find a quiet place and ask God to lead this process. Don't just ask "What do I want?" Ask "Lord, what are You inviting me into? What would bring You glory through my life? Where do I best fit in Your plan?"

Write your prayer down. Pray it out loud and silently multiple times, until you're ready to start plotting your course. This one step changes everything.

- Commit your work to the Lord, and your plans will be established.
  —Proverbs 16:3 ESV

- As you pray, remind yourself that Kingdom-driven goals start with surrender, not just ambition.

STEP 2: FIND YOUR SPACE

Get somewhere quiet.

- Put your phone away.
- Shutdown your computer.
- Turn off the television.

Give yourself uninterrupted time. This isn't a five-minute exercise—give it the time it deserves. Feel free to take as long as you want. Come back to it again and again if needed. Take an hour. Take a day. Take a weekend if you need to. This is your life we're talking about.

STEP 3: WRITE YOUR TOP 50 GOALS

Start writing—anything that comes to mind. Don't filter. Don't edit. Don't overthink it. Just write down everything you want to do, see, experience, accomplish, and become. Dream BIG and dream BOLD.

Tactical Tip 1: When you work through this goal-setting process, please know that it doesn't have to be fancy. You don't need a detailed spreadsheet. All you need is a piece of paper to write on. And as soon as a goal pops in your head, jot it down on the line directly below the one above it.

Tactical Tip 2: This may be the most important thing to remember. The goals that you write down in this mission are not the goals that you "think" you can accomplish, but the goals you "want" to accomplish. All the goals you would love to see come to fruition. The goals that, if achieved, would make you feel like you've accomplished everything you've wanted to accomplish, ever since you were a boy.

Write down the house on the beach you've always dreamt of owning (or maybe that's just me). The places you want to travel. The things you want to learn. The relationships you want to build. The businesses you want to start. The books you want to read or write. The skills you want to develop.

You need **BIG** goals and **small** goals. Write them all down:

- Places you want to go
- Things you want to learn (golf, archery, juggling, an instrument, a language)
- Experiences you want to have
- Financial goals
- Health and fitness goals
- Spiritual goals
- Family and relationship goals
- Career and business goals
- Things you want to give or contribute
- The impact you want to make on others
- The man you want to become

STEP 4: SORT BY TIMELINE

Once your list is written, go back and mark each goal with a timeframe:

- **1 Year** - Goals you want to accomplish in the next 12 months.
- **3 Years** - Goals that you think will take more time and planning.
- **10 Years** – These are your biggest, boldest, and longest-range vision goals.

Here's a quick example of what yours may look like:

- Get in shape – 1
- Grow closer to God – 1
- Lock down a daily Bible/prayer routine – 1
- Start a new side hustle – 3
- Learn how to play the guitar – 10
- Run a marathon – 3
- Pay off my mortgage – 10
- Save some cash – 1
- Get a new truck – 3
- Be more present with my family – 1
- Start a new business – 1
- Go on a vacation to Hawaii – 3
- Go to Europe – 3
- Visit Israel – 10
- Get that job promotion – 3
- Start a new career – 3
- Take an online training course – 1
- Get clear on my true calling – 1
- Pick up a new hobby – 1

- Start or join a men's group – 1
- Own my dream home -10
- Learn to speak a foreign language – 3
- Be debt-free – 10
- Read a new book – 1
- Read 5 to 10 books – 3
- Write a book – 5
- Start a family – 3

STEP 5: TAKE MASSIVE ACTION

Dreams without action are just wishes. Pick your most important goal right now and identify your next move. What's one specific action you can take today? You don't have to complete the whole thing at once—just take one step that moves you forward.

Then keep moving. Every step forward creates momentum. Every small win compounds into something bigger. Don't stress if things don't happen right away. Stay committed. Stay focused. Stay in motion.

And give yourself some affirmation along the way. Remind yourself that you can do this. That God is with you (Genesis 28:15). Make a promise to yourself that you're never going to quit. That you're going to keep growing, keep advancing, and keep becoming the man God created you to be.

Because the man who keeps moving—even slowly—will always outpace the man who never starts.

STEP 6: BUILD IN SPIRITUAL CHECKPOINTS

Goals drift when prayer disappears. Schedule regular check-ins with God:

- **Weekly** – A quick check: Am I still on course?
- **Monthly** – Review your goals in prayer.
- **Quarterly** – Reassess: Lord, am I still aligned?

Sometimes the goal stays the same. Sometimes God adjusts the route. Sometimes He changes the destination entirely. Regardless, stay flexible and yielded to His will—not your own.

STEP 7: CELEBRATE EVERY WIN

When you complete a goal—big or small—go back to your list. Cross it off. Write the date you completed it. Pat yourself on the back. Treat yourself and your loved ones to something nice. Then pause. Give thanks. Acknowledge God's hand in it. Your gratitude will keep pride at bay and invite a deeper trust in the Lord.

STEP 8: KEEP ADDING

Your list is never finished. It's evergreen. Always changing. As you grow, your goals will grow. Keep adding. Keep dreaming. Keep advancing.

STEP 9: STAY ON COURSE

Review your goals regularly. Check your heading. Make adjustments. Don't let life drift you off track. And if someone or something pushes you off course, correct it immediately. The longer you drift, the harder it is to get back on track.

MISSION TOOLS

- **A journal or notebook.** Write your goals down. Something about putting pen to paper makes your goals more real and more achievable.
- **Your Bible**. Let God's Word shape your vision. Pray over your goals. Ask God what He wants for your life and write down what He shows you.
- **A trusted friend or mentor**. Share your goals with someone who will encourage you and hold you accountable.
- **A willing and surrendered heart**. Be open to where God leads. Hold your plans loosely and trust Him with the outcome. The best goals are the ones that God breathes life into.
- ***Special Ops for Men* Resources**. For additional tools to help you stay on course, visit:

  JeffJerina.com / Books / SpecialOpsforMen / Resources

ESTIMATED COMPLETION TIME

1 hour to several days.

Give this mission the time it deserves. Don't rush it. You can start in five minutes, but your best work will come when you carve out strategic, focused time. This isn't a task to check off once you've written your goals down—it's a course to chart and continually check throughout your lifetime.

MISSION FUEL

Delight yourself also in the Lord, and He shall give you the desires of your heart.
—Psalm 37:4

Commit your work to the Lord, and your plans will be established.
—Proverbs 16:3 ESV

A man's heart plans his way, but the Lord directs his steps.
—Proverbs 16:9

For I know the plans I have for you, declares the Lord, plans to prosper you and not to harm you, plans to give you hope and a future.
—Jeremiah 29:11 NIV

Write the vision and make it plain on tablets, so he may run who reads it.
—Habakkuk 2:2

You were *not* made to drift.

You were made to move with purpose, live with intention, and leave a legacy that outlasts you.

The devil knows what you're capable of. That's why he's dead set on keeping you distracted and discouraged. He wants your dreams buried so deep that you forget they ever existed. And he wants your full potential sitting on the shelf, collecting dust, never deployed.

Don't give him that ground.

Not one inch.

Plot your course. Write it down. Pray over it like your life depends on it—because in many ways, it does. Commit it to God. And then move—boldly, faithfully, and without apology—toward the life He designed for you to live.

Because the world needs the man you're becoming.

Your family needs the man you're becoming.

And somewhere down the line, your grandchildren will tell the story of a man who didn't settle. A man who didn't drift. A man who was locked in and never let go.

That man is you.

Now go—plot your course, commit it to God, and advance.

You've got this. Now go get it!

MISSION DEBRIEF

Well done, soldier! Mission accomplished. You started or completely finished charting your course today. Now let's assess what you've done:

1. What did you pray before you started the mission?

2. What are your top three goals for the next year?

3. What is your boldest ten-year goal?

4. What has kept you from setting goals in the past?

5. What did this mission reveal about what you truly want from life?

6. Who will you share your goals with to stay accountable?

7. On a scale of 1 to 10 (10 being the clearest), how clear is your course right now?

8. What is the first action you will take today or tomorrow toward your most important goal?

9. How will you keep God at the center of this process going forward?

10. What would it mean for your loved ones if you actually achieved everything you wrote down—and when you stand before God, what do you hope you had the courage to pursue?

FINAL MISSION DEBRIEF

This part of the book is where you zoom out, take a bird's eye view of all the Special Ops missions you've completed so far. I hope that by the time you've reached this section, you've completed every mission (at least once). If you find that there is a question that wasn't included in this final briefing, feel free to add it as you deem necessary. If some of these questions seem too deep or too difficult to answer, don't sweat it, simply answer each one as best you can. There are no right or wrong answers here. Alright, soldier, let's get started!

1. What was the biggest win you experienced?

2. Where did you struggle the most—and why?

3. What thought patterns or behaviors did you capture and take captive throughout these missions?

4. What Scripture or truth had the most impact on you?

5. What distractions or "enemy tactics" tried to derail you, and how did you respond?

6. How did these missions bring you closer to God?

7. What would you do differently if you had to complete these missions again?

8. How will you apply what you learned to your daily life or next mission?

9. Who can you encourage or lead by sharing what you learned in this mission?

10. What's a mission that you're ready to complete again, or one that wasn't listed in this book and that you would like to roll out?

YOUR MISSION CONTINUES

If you've made it this far, one of two things is true: you completed all 15 missions—or you're here early because you want to know what's ahead.

Either way, I'm glad you're here.

And if you completed every mission, congratulations. That alone separates you from the crowd. Most men start things. Few men finish. Even fewer actually execute. You did. And that's not average—that's elite.

Completing these missions doesn't make you perfect. But it does make you battle-tested. It marks you as a man who shows up, follows through, and refuses to quit.

You've earned the title: **Special Ops Warrior.**

But understand this: earning the title isn't the goal. Living it is.

As I mentioned in the Introduction, this was never just about reading pages. It was about having a gameplan—a cohesive battle strategy for your life.

Every mission you executed was deliberate. Every debrief was intentional. Every page was designed to strengthen your faith and transform how you live.

Now comes the hard part: sustained execution.

Go back and complete any missions you haven't finished. Repeat the ones that challenged you most. Refine them as you grow. When one mission strengthens you, find or build another one that stretches you further.

Debrief. Adjust. Re-engage.

Review your 1-year objectives.
Strengthen your 3-year strategy.
Expand your 10-year vision.

Then move.

The battlefield is always there.
Complacency is still the enemy.
Drift is still the threat.

You are not finished.

You are deployed.

STANDING ORDERS

- 3 Complete each (if you haven't already).
- Conduct your personal debriefs.
- Review and refine your goals regularly.
- Launch new missions as you grow.
- Train another man and multiply your impact.

Special force operators don't dabble. They execute, assess, and improve. That's your standard now, too.

REINFORCEMENTS & ADVANCED TRAINING

Ready to operate at an even higher level?

Report to the **Resources area** at **JeffJerina.com/Books/SpecialOpsforMen/Resources** to gear up with these free tools:

- Download the Special Ops Warrior Code
- Access three additional missions
- Deploy the Mission Tracker and Battle Plan
- Join the Special Ops Brotherhood—men just like you who refuse to settle for mediocrity

Remember:

- Isolation weakens.
- Brotherhood strengthens.
- No elite unit operates alone. And neither should you.

You were never made for defeat. You were forged for victory—to love God fiercely, make Him known boldly, and lead with honor and love. Not perfectly, but faithfully.

Now move out. Your mission continues.

This is not a finish line—it's deployment.

Mission status: ongoing.

Stay sharp. Stay disciplined. Stay anchored in Christ.

Fighting alongside you,

Jeff

WAR ROOM

GROUP STUDY GUIDE

Every mission in this book was built for solo work. No team required.

That hasn't changed.

But after you've completed them, sitting down with other men who did the same multiplies the impact. You sharpen each other. You call out blind spots. You build brotherhood.

The requirements? Minimal.

You don't need a leader or an expert.
You don't even need a perfect plan.

All you need is a few men who are serious about growing.

Once you've assembled your team, use these questions to talk honestly. Share wins. Share struggles. Hold each other accountable. Then execute.

MISSION 1: RECHARGE YOUR BATTERY

1. How did spending time in God's Word affect you this week?
2. What's one thing you can change to make this mission a more consistent part of your life?
3. How can others help you stay committed to this?

MISSION 2: ARM YOURSELF WITH TRUTH

1. What part of the verse you memorized hit you the hardest?
2. What surprised you about this mission?
3. Was there a moment this week when the verse helped you in real time? If so, describe it.

MISSION 3: LOCK IN GOD'S WORD

1. How did slowing down and actually thinking about God's Word impact you?
2. What's a difficulty or struggle this mission has helped you with?
3. What verse do you want to meditate on next, and what situation are you taking it into?

MISSION 4: CEASE FIRE

1. Before this mission, when was the last time you were completely still?
2. What did you hear from God that you wouldn't have heard if you stayed busy?
3. How would this change your life if you did this on a more consistent basis?

MISSION 5: CLEAR THE DEBRIS

1. How long have you been carrying this weight?
2. What has this sin cost you or stolen from you—time, peace, relationships—and how will you get it back?
3. When temptation hits again, what weapon will you use to fight it?

MISSION 6: MASTER YOUR MINDSET

1. Where do you see the enemy attacking your thoughts most right now? *Faith, identity, pride, leadership, lust, or some other area?*
2. How would your life be different if you consistently chose God's truth over that specific lie?
3. What's one practical way you can guard your mind this week?

MISSION 7: ARMOR UP

1. What's been keeping you from challenging yourself like this in the past?

2. What does the way you've been training your body say about the way you've been living your life?
3. How can someone else (or the men in this group) help you stay committed going forward?

MISSION 8: GO DARK

1. What did this mission reveal about what normally controls your time and attention?
2. What additional boundaries or parameters do you need to set in place the next time you "Go Dark"?
3. Why do you think this mission is so hard for men to complete—let alone start?

MISSION 9: SHARPEN YOUR EDGE

1. What did you learn to sharpen your edge? How can this new skill or knowledge give you an advantage in your everyday life?
2. What's something new you'd like to learn or get better at to help you sharpen your edge even more?
3. What advice or insight would you share with another man to help him complete this mission successfully?

MISSION 10: EMBRACE DISCOMFORT

1. What was one thing you learned about yourself as a result of this mission?
2. What obstacle (internal or external) did you confront during this mission?

3. What area in your life do you need to keep leaning into discomfort?

MISSION 11: DEPLOY GENEROSITY

1. Did this mission change or challenge the way you think about generosity? Explain.
2. Why do you think generosity feels risky for so many men?
3. What is one area of your life where God may be calling you to give more boldly right now?

MISSION 12: INVEST IN WHAT MATTERS

1. What was your biggest takeaway about yourself and the importance of investing in others?
2. Why do you think it's easier to stay busy than to be fully present with someone?
3. How could intentionally investing in others reshape your relationships now and in the future?

MISSION 13: BUILD YOUR BROTHERHOOD

1. Was being the one who reached out first tough for you? Why do you think that is?
2. Why do men often wait for someone else to make the first move?
3. How can we build a brotherhood where every man is supported, strengthened, and honored?

MISSION 14: HONOR THE CALL

1. Why do you think sharing your faith is so difficult, even when you know it's true?
2. How does seeing yourself as Christ's ambassador, called to the Great Commission, change the way you approach each day?
3. How can we encourage one another to speak up about Jesus instead of staying silent?

MISSION 15: PLOT YOUR COURSE

1. Which of your goals are you most excited about? Which one do you think scares or gives you the most doubt that you'll actually accomplish? Why?
2. How do they align with what God is calling you to?
3. How can this group push you, hold you accountable, or support you as you work towards these goals?

RESOURCES

In this section, you'll find a collection of tools and resources to help you live like a Special Ops soldier. Some of these resources I've already mentioned in this book, while others are additional materials designed to help you grow in your faith, career, or personal life. Each item includes a link to access or download the resource directly. For even faster access, scan one of the QR codes on the last page of this section using your phone's camera app—each code will take you straight to the corresponding page on my website at **JeffJerina.com**.

MISSION TRACKER + BATTLE PLAN

- JeffJerina.com/Books/SpecialOpsforMen/Resources

SPECIAL OPS WARRIOR CODE

- JeffJerina.com/Books/SpecialOpsforMen/Resources

3 BONUS SPECIAL OPS MISSIONS

- JeffJerina.com/Books/SpecialOpsforMen/Resources

THE JEFF JERINA SHOW PODCAST

- JeffJerina.com/Podcast *(audio and video)*

THE IGNITE NEWSLETTER

- JeffJerina.com/Newsletter

FAITH & LIFE ALIGNMENT TOOL

- JeffJerina.com/Faith-and-Life-Alignment-Assessment

PURPOSE & CALLING PAGE

- JeffJerina.com/Purpose

DISCOVER YOUR PERSONALITY TYPE

- JeffJerina.com/DISCProfile

THE SUCCESS BLUEPRINT

- JeffJerina.com/SuccessBlueprint

MY OTHER BOOKS

- JeffJerina.com/Books

MY ONLINE COURSES

- JeffJerina.com/Courses

BUSINESS & PERSONAL GROWTH COACHING

- JeffJerina.com/Training

PODCAST COACHING

- JeffJerina.com/Podcast-Coaching

MY SPEAKING PAGE

- JeffJerina.com/Speaking

JOIN MY AFFILIATE PROGRAM

- JeffJerina.com/Affiliate

ADDITIONAL FREE TOOLS

- JeffJerina.com/Resources

Use the QR Codes to access the specific page below:

MY HOMEPAGE
JeffJerina.com

SPECIAL OPS FOR MEN RESOURCES

NOTES

MISSION 8

Digital marketers report that people: Jerina, Jeff. *Cut Through the Noise*. (Wylie, TX: Olive Tree Publications, 2021) 91.

Because let's be honest—the noises aren't getting: Jerina, Jeff. *Cut Through the Noise*. (Wylie, TX: Olive Tree Publications, 2021) 27.

Studies reveal that men spend an average of: Jerina, Jeff. *Cut Through the Noise*. (Wylie, TX: Olive Tree Publications, 2021) 41.

The more we are distracted by earthly things: Jerina, Jeff. *Cut Through the Noise*. (Wylie, TX: Olive Tree Publications, 2021) 38.

Don't settle for a life that's: Jerina, Jeff. *Cut Through the Noise*. (Wylie, TX: Olive Tree Publications, 2021) 166.

MISSION 9

James Allen said it best: Allen, James. *As a Man Thinketh*. 1903.

MISSION 14

In fact, research shows that 98% of Christians: Jerina, Jeff. *Faith Without Fear: How to Share What You Believe with Confidence and Power*. (Wylie, TX: Olive Tree Publications, 2019, p. 24.

For more on why Christian men must share their faith and the staggering statistics about evangelism, see *Faith Without Fear* at JeffJerina.com/Books/FaithWithoutFear

ACKNOWLEDGMENTS

Thank you to the amazing teams at SiteSpartan.com and Olive Tree Publications for your hard work and dedication throughout the writing of this book. Your patience and attention to detail with the book cover and interior formatting have been spot on.

Thank you to my brothers-in-arms, true warriors of the faith, John Christian and Steve Fedyski, for your timely prayers, honest feedback, and encouragement throughout my journey of writing this book.

Thank you to my wife and children for being part of my life and for sharing this journey with me.

To my daughter, never forget that you are strong, beautiful, and deeply loved by God. He has given you courage, purpose, creativity, and the innate ability to step into a story and bring it to life. That gift is powerful. I am proud of you, and I love you.

To my son, you are a warrior for Jesus Christ. The strength, skill, and discipline you show already reveal the man God is shaping you to become. A special ops soldier in God's kingdom—you are set apart for a purpose. I am proud of you, and I love you.

Thank You, Jesus—my Lord and Savior—for saving my life, not just physically but spiritually. You have called me into Your service and entrusted me with a mission.

ABOUT THE AUTHOR

Jeff Jerina is a speaker, author, podcaster, coach, evangelist, and faith-driven entrepreneur whose mission is to help people strengthen, share, and live out their Christian faith with passion and purpose.

After battling severe depression, suicidal thoughts, and a life-threatening form of OCD known as body dysmorphic disorder for four years—and enduring a corporate layoff—Jeff encountered the life-transforming power of the gospel. Through his faith in Jesus, his life was redirected, his hope was restored, and given a new calling to help others do the same.

Jeff is the host of *The Jeff Jerina Show*, a globally ranked Christian podcast. He is the author of multiple books, including *Cut Through the Noise* and *Faith Without Fear*, as well as *A Prodigal's Journey*, a poem reflecting his spiritual journey. He has served as an adjunct seminary professor and, with a BBA in Management and a Master's in Biblical Studies, is able to reach and communicate with a wide variety of audiences.

He is the founder and CEO of SiteSpartan.com, a website design, hosting, and digital marketing company, and of ChristmasLightsDesign.com, a professional holiday light installation, training, and wholesale supplier. He is also a professional tennis coach, an honorary inductee of *Who's Who in America,* and has performed juggling routines for large audiences, including on an international cruise.

Through his speaking, coaching, consulting, writing, online courses, and digital ministry, Jeff equips individuals, churches, schools, and businesses to strengthen their faith, share their message, and achieve personal and professional growth.

Jeff and his wife live in Texas with their two children.

To explore his courses, books, podcast, free resources, and to subscribe to Jeff's email newsletter, visit:

- JeffJerina.com

To book Jeff for a speaking or training event, visit:

- JeffJerina.com/Speaking
  or email Jeff@JeffJerina.com

CONTACT JEFF

For the latest *Special Ops for Men* updates, visit:

- JeffJerina.com/Books/SpecialOpsforMen

To explore *Special Ops for Men* gear and join the online community, visit:

- JeffJerina.com/Books/SpecialOpsforMen/Resources

For more information on Jeff's other books, visit:

- JeffJerina.com/Books

For online training courses, visit:

- JeffJerina.com/Courses

To listen to *The Jeff Jerina Show* podcast, visit:

- JeffJerina.com/Podcast

To book Jeff for a speaking or training event, visit:

- JeffJerina.com/Speaking

To work with Jeff in coaching or consulting, visit:

- JeffJerina.com/Training

To purchase bulk copies of any book at a discount or for other inquiries, visit:

- JeffJerina.com/Contact
  or email Jeff@JeffJerina.com

DON'T LET THIS BE THE END

Join the IGNITE Newsletter for weekly encouragement, biblical wisdom, leadership insight, and practical tools to help you personally and professionally.

You'll get all the updates about upcoming podcast episodes, videos, inspirational quotes, and books I think you may like, as well as tips, tricks, and bonus information from my books, courses, and the Special Ops community directly in your inbox... all on a variety of topics that are geared to help you go the next level in your faith, life, and career.

Join Now at:

- JeffJerina.com/Newsletter

CUT THROUGH THE NOISE

4 Steps to Joy, Peace, and Freedom

Discover a Simple Way to Eliminate Hurry, Remove Distractions, and Connect with God…

Cut Through the Noise guides you through four practical steps to remove distractions, reclaim your time, and live with deeper peace and presence. Endorsed by top Christian leaders, this book will help you GET BACK YOUR LIFE! Plus, you'll also get these bonuses:

- **BONUS #1:** FREE Life Map
- **BONUS #2:** FREE Additional Resources
- **BONUS #3:** FREE Audio from top leaders

Available in digital, audio, and print formats at:
JeffJerina.com/Books/Cut-Through-the-Noise

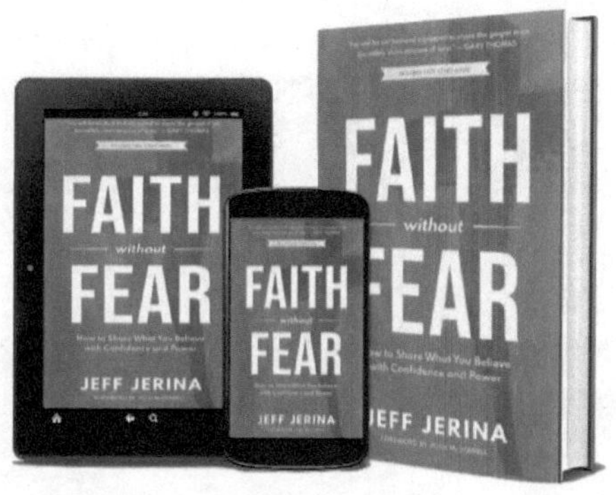

FAITH WITHOUT FEAR

How to Share What You Believe
with Confidence and Power

Discover the Simple, Natural Way to Share the Gospel in Everyday Conversations…

No matter your age, vocation, or biblical knowledge, you'll learn how to naturally share Jesus with anyone at any time. Endorsed by top Christian leaders, this book shows you how to confidently and naturally share your faith—without being afraid, feeling pressured, or sounding awkward.

- **BONUS #1:** Sharing the Gospel Game Plan
- **BONUS #2:** Discussion Questions
- **BONUS #3:** Role-playing Sections

Available in digital, audio, and print formats at:
JeffJerina.com/Books/FaithWithoutFear

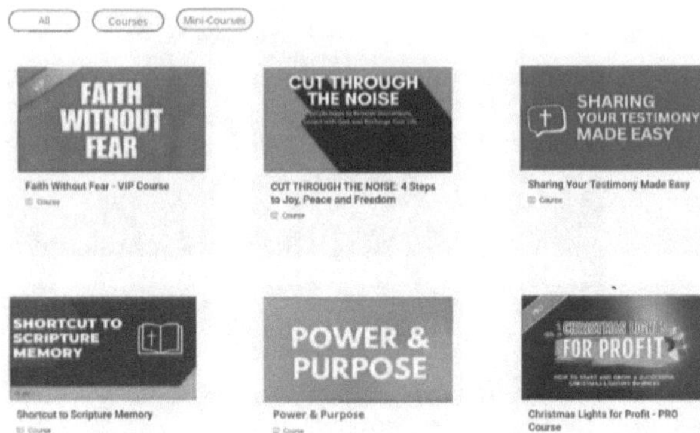

ONLINE COURSES

Simple. Strategic. Mission-Ready.

Practical, Impactful Courses That Get the Job Done.

Whether you want to grow spiritually, strengthen your leadership, build a business, or boldly live out your faith, these online trainings equip you with clear steps and practical strategies you can apply immediately. To help you focus your growth, my courses are strategically organized into three core areas:

- **Personal & Spiritual Growth**
- **Leadership & Team Development**
- **Business & Entrepreneurship**

Learn more and enroll today at:
JeffJerina.com/Courses

FAITH AND LIFE ALIGNMENT

Discover Where You're Thriving—and Where God is Calling You Higher.

A Free, 5-minute Check to Evaluate How Your Daily Life Reflects Your Faith in 7 Key Areas

This assessment will help you evaluate how closely your daily life reflects your faith in 7 key areas—including your priorities, purpose, mindset, relationships, and habits. You'll receive a personalized Faith & Life Alignment Report with insights, encouragement, and practical next steps you can apply immediately. The Faith and Life Alignment Assessment Includes:

- **Instant Results**
- **Scripture-based Insights**
- **Practical Next Steps**

Learn more and enroll today at:
JeffJerina.com/Faith-and-Life-Alignment-Assessment

THE JEFF JERINA SHOW PODCAST

Weekly Interviews, Strategy, and Advice to Help You Grow in Life, Faith, and Business.

The Jeff Jerina Show features meaningful conversations with high-performers, Christian entrepreneurs, faith leaders, authors, athletes, and everyday overcomers who share real stories, life lessons, and defining moments. Jeff also shares his own insights, strategies, and practical advice to help you grow spiritually, personally, and professionally.

Tune in to gain wisdom, encouragement, and actionable steps so you can become the best version of you.

Listen and Subscribe at:
JeffJerina.com/Podcast

SPECIAL OPS COMMUNITY

Iron Sharpens Iron

Live Bold. Lead Strong. Stand Firm.

Join a community of men committed to accountability, discipline, leadership, and honor.

No spectators.
No social media.
No distractions.
Just men sharpening men—pushing each other to grow spiritually, mentally, and physically, and to live with purpose in every area of life.

This is your team. Your brotherhood. Your next mission.

Join the Brotherhood at:
JeffJerina.com/Books/SpecialOpsforMen/Resources

COACHING & SPEAKING

Jeff has a passion for helping men, women, and youth strengthen their faith and grow in every area of life through his keynotes, workshops, and coaching. He speaks on topics ranging from his personal faith journey, leadership, faith-driven entrepreneurship, evangelism, men's ministry, and overcoming challenges like depression, OCD, and body image issues. Jeff also provides coaching for personal growth, business strategy, podcasting, and ministry development.

Book Jeff for Speaking or Coaching:

- **Speaking:**
  JeffJerina.com/Speaking
- **Podcast Coaching:**
  JeffJerina.com/Podcast-Coaching
- **Personal/Business Coaching:**
  JeffJerina.com/Training

DOWNLOAD YOUR BONUS GEAR FREE!

To say thank you for buying this book, I want to give you some exclusive bonus gear—100% FREE.

This gear is reserved for readers only. It's not available anywhere else. You'll receive:

- **Mission Tracker & Battle Plan** - A tactical tool to track your objectives, progress, and wins.
- **Special Ops Warrior Code** - A bold declaration to anchor your identity and what you stand for.

TO DOWNLOAD, GO TO:

JeffJerina.com/Books/SpecialOpsforMen/Resources

URGENT PLEA!

Thank You for Reading My Book!

I'm so grateful you took the time to read this book, and I truly value your feedback. Your input helps me improve future editions, online trainings, and upcoming books.

Please leave a helpful review on Amazon to let me know what you thought of *Special Ops for Men*. Your review helps other men strengthen their faith, stand strong, and live with purpose.

Submit your review through this link:

- https://JeffJerina.com/SpecialOpsReview

Thank you!

Jeff

www.ingramcontent.com/pod-product-compliance
Lightning Source LLC
LaVergne TN
LVHW090515110826
845146LV00003B/859